The Reddick
C# Style Guide

Greg Reddick

Best practices for writing C# code

The Reddick C# Style Guide
Best practices for writing C# code

Published by:
Xoc Software
Kenmore, WA
http://www.xoc.net

Send correspondence about this work to g-bestpractices@xoc.net.

First publication date: 2015-11-12

Revision date: 2015-12-01

Print edition ISBN: 978-0-692-53174-7

Amazon Kindle ASIN: B018HGOZ1I

For Sandi

CONTENTS

PREFACE

The Reddick C# Style Guide provides a guideline for writing Microsoft .NET code using C#. The practices that follow come from programming in C# since its creation, and over 35 years of programming overall. These practices are constructed using conventions established by Microsoft, as well as the examples of .NET code presented by the .NET help, tools such as Code Analysis and StyleCop, the public interface of the .NET Framework, and many other resources.

I am the author of the most widely used naming conventions for Visual Basic and Visual Basic for Applications (VBA): *The Reddick VBA Naming Conventions* and *The Reddick VBA Coding Conventions*. Although *The Reddick C# Style Guide* has little in common with the VBA conventions, I learned many things in gathering consensus and publishing those conventions that I have put to use here. I have established the practices used by teams using other languages (such as C) as well. I have been concerned with the quality and consistency of code for my entire Software Engineering career.

I have reviewed many other sets of conventions and best practices for .NET and other languages and programming environments. Where possible, I try to adopt the consensus of these recommendations. Where conflicts occur between these other sources, I have chosen the technique that I have found is the easiest to implement and maintain. This book provides a concise but complete set of rules for a single programmer or a development team. It is organized in a way that makes it easy to find the rules that apply to the code you are actively writing.

I comment on these conventions and other topics on my blog: http://blog.xoc.net.

I hope that you will find *The Reddick C# Style Guide* useful.

How to Read This Book

Read the Introduction and General Information sections at the beginning of the book. These give the foundation for the rules that follow. The Coding Conventions are the main part of the book and are a reference. You will want to read these quickly once, but come back to the specific relevant topics as you write code. Some sections at the end have general best practices that you will want to review. The appendices have some lists, checklist, and alternatives to these rules that you will want to consider. There is also an extensive code example showing these rules in use.

Greg Reddick

INTRODUCTION

A foolish consistency is the hobgoblin of little minds, adored by little statesmen and philosophers and divines. With consistency a great soul has simply nothing to do. He may as well concern himself with his shadow on the wall. Speak what you think now in hard words, and to-morrow speak what to-morrow thinks in hard words again, though it contradict every thing you said to-day. — 'Ah, so you shall be sure to be misunderstood.' — Is it so bad, then, to be misunderstood? Pythagoras was misunderstood, and Socrates, and Jesus, and Luther, and Copernicus, and Galileo, and Newton, and every pure and wise spirit that ever took flesh. To be great is to be misunderstood.

Ralph Waldo Emerson

In writing prose, being misunderstood might lead to greatness, but having a computer or other programmers misunderstand what the code is attempting to accomplish leads to problems. There is nothing foolish about being consistent when writing code. The practices described here can have real impact on the performance, security, and quality of the code, frequently working with subtleties of C# and the .NET Framework of which the average programmer may be unaware.

Best Practices

The paper *Best Practices Research: A Methodological Guide for the Perplexed* defines the term:

The Term "best practice" implies that it is best when compared to any other alternative course of action and that it is a practice designed to achieve some deliberative end.

In the terms of producing programs for .NET, the methods and techniques described in this book are the best practices for one or more reasons:

- They provide more secure code. For example, not providing a strong name on an assembly allows silent modifications to the assembly. The best practice of requiring a strong name on an assembly guarantees that the strong name uniquely identifies the assembly.

- They provide code that performs better and consumes fewer resources. For example, an object that includes a empty finalizer must go through two garbage collections before it is removed from memory. The best practices prohibit empty finalizers.

- They provide better quality code. As a simple and obvious example, C# allows two different methods with names differing only by case (for example, SomeMethod and Somemethod); however, doing so can be very confusing to programmers who might call the wrong one. Furthermore, if publicly visible and placed into a library, one of these methods will not be accessible to Visual Basic, which is case insensitive. The best practice of avoiding methods that differ only by case provides better quality code.

- They provide code that is more consistent. Being consistent allows understanding the code at a more rapid rate, especially when more than one programmer is working on the code. This allows new programmers to come onto the team and get up to speed faster. Being consistent allows programmers to understand the code without having to learn the conventions of the programmer who wrote it. It reduces the number of bugs introduced into the code. For example, while the rule for capitalizing a variable in camel case may be somewhat arbitrary (a variable could just as well be capitalized as enableAction, EnableAction, or ENABLEACTION), being consistent in the capitalization makes the code easier to read and maintain. A programmer seeing a variable in camel case knows that it will not be exposed beyond the current scope.

Typographic Conventions

Rules are denoted with a ✻ symbol.

✻ This is a rule.

A rule may be followed by comments with:

- A more detailed description of the rule

- How the rule is applied

- The reasoning for the rule's existence

A rule may have exceptions where the rule does not apply, denoted with the ⊗ symbol. This shows an exception:

⊗ This describes an exception to the rule.

Most rules will have examples of properly implementing the rule, denoted with the ✓ symbol. This shows an example

```
✓ Do this.
```

The code examples shown are meant to be just enough to demonstrate a correct way of writing the particular rule. They will not show the required XML comments unless the example is specifically about implementing XML comments. They may omit the required using statements for the namespaces in use, replace some code by a comment, or omit error handling.

The code examples are written to be compatible with C# version 5 to be applicable to the widest code base currently in use. A few examples could be written slightly more efficiently using the syntax introduced in C# version 6. Except where explicitly noted, none of these affects the point being demonstrated by the code example.

There frequently are also counterexamples of things not to use, denoted with the ✗ symbol. This shows a counterexample:

```
✗  Do not do this.
```

Counterexample code may violate other rules in addition to the rule being demonstrated.

Code Analysis or StyleCop may enforce a rule. These rules are denoted with the ▶ symbol. This shows a StyleCop rule that enforces the given rule:

▶ StyleCop SA1000

The correspondence of the rules given here and Code Analysis and StyleCop rules may not be one-to-one. A rule given here may be broader the Code Analysis or StyleCop rule, so they may only catch some violations. There may also be more than one rule given here that are all caught by one Code Analysis or StyleCop rule.

C# Terminology

Terms such as white space, member, element, type, and so forth, throughout this book are defined in the C# Language Specification. Version 5 of that document can be found at this address: https://www.microsoft.com/en-us/download/details.aspx?id=7029.

Requirement Terminology

All rules are written in a format using certain keywords that designate how strongly the rule is to be applied. Some rules must always be adhered to, whereas others may have some circumstances where they may be ignored. Some are merely suggestions.

The key words **"must"**, **"must not"**, **"required"**, **"shall"**, **"shall not"**, **"should"**, **"should not"**, **"recommended"**, **"may"**, and **"optional"**, when in bold face, are to be interpreted using the definitions in RFC 2119. (https://tools.ietf.org/html/rfc2119).

Must: This word, or the terms **"required"** or **"shall"**, means that the rule is an absolute requirement. Any exceptions to the requirement will be explicitly enumerated in the following text.

Must not: This phrase, or the phrase **"shall not"**, means that the rule is an absolute prohibition. Any exceptions to the requirement will be explicitly enumerated in the following text.

Should: This word, or the adjective **"recommended"**, means that there may exist valid reasons in particular circumstances to ignore a particular rule, but the full implications must be understood and carefully weighed before choosing a different course.

Should not: This phrase, or the phrase **"not recommended"** means that there may exist valid reasons in particular circumstances when the particular behavior is acceptable or even useful, but the full implications should be understood and the case carefully weighed before implementing any behavior described with this label.

May: This word, or the adjective **"optional"**, means that an item is truly optional.

GENERAL INFORMATION

This section describes some general information necessary before entering into discussion of how to code particular elements in C#.

Adopting Best Practices

The rules given here are suggestions. In any given organization, there may be reasons to alter these rules. Some organizations, for example, may find a maximum line length of 100 characters is more useful than the 140 characters given here, or may want to indent using spaces rather than tabs. In most cases, it is more important to have all of the programmers use the same practices than the specific practices they use.

If a practice is altered, it should be documented, made available to all programmers on the development team, and the justification for the alteration recorded for posterity. Five years down the road, it may be difficult to remember reasoning behind the alteration, and the people who made the decision may have left the company.

These rules assume that the programmers are writing in English. If there is another primary language, then modification to certain of the rules are necessary, particularly the rules regarding the text of XML comments, to match the language of the programming team.

Programmers tend to have strongly voiced opinions about the coding style they want to use. A specific programmer may not agree with the practices listed here. In any group of programmers, having them all completely agree on a coding style is as unlikely as having them all agree on their politics or religion. A group of programmers may spend weeks arguing about the rules and not getting any work done. Adopting a set of practices is best handled by having management consult with the programming team (possibly with a very small Best Practices committee), but then impose the practices to be used on the team.

Appendix D: Alternate Choices lists some common alternate choices that a programming team might make over the style given here.

Code Quality Tools: Code Analysis and StyleCop

There are several tools to help enforce the creation of good quality code: Code Analysis and StyleCop. These tools check the quality of the code in a project and flag implementations that are not recommended, although legally allowed by the compiler. Many of the rules provided here follow the rules established by Code Analysis and StyleCop.

Visual Studio provides a built-in tool called Code Analysis. Code Analysis is run from the Analyze menu in Visual Studio. It can also be configured in the Project Properties to run after every compile. Code Analysis uses modifiable rules sets to control what rules it checks.

Microsoft originally implemented the rules in Code Analysis in an external tool called FxCop. FxCop works by performing reflection on the .NET assembly, which means that it cannot analyze details that are not in the Intermediate Language stored in the assembly. Since comments, indenting, private variable names, and other details are lost in the compilation process, FxCop rules cannot comment on them. Starting with Visual Studio 2012, Microsoft abandoned development on the separate FxCop tool, and incorporated its functionality into Visual Studio as Code Analysis.

Visual Studio 2015 added a new concept: analyzers. The Roslyn compiler included with Visual Studio 2015 allows deep analysis of the code. The analyzers provide a plug-in way of providing rules to Visual Studio. Unlike FxCop, these can operate on the source code, not just the compiled assembly, and can provide warnings on details that are lost in the compilation process. Rule violations show immediately in the Visual Studio code window, without compiling the code. Furthermore, these rules can provide an interface to fix the code, not just report warnings about it. The Visual Studio 2015 Code Analysis rules are still based on the FxCop rules, but in the future Microsoft will likely add rules that report problems only detectable in the source code.

Because FxCop and Code Analysis could only report problems with the compiled assembly, Microsoft created another tool that analyzed the source code: StyleCop. StyleCop parses the C# source code and reported issues with the style. Since it works on the source code and not the compiled assembly, it can complain about comments, line breaks, private variables, and other stylistic issues. It also allows writing custom rules to supplement the rules that it provides. With the advent of analyzers in Visual Studio 2015, StyleCop has been re-implemented as a set of analyzer rules.

Find instructions on installing StyleCop in various versions of Visual Studio at http://blog.xoc.net/2015/10/installing-stylecop-in-visual-studio.html.

Over time, more analyzers will be developed for Visual Studio that will check various aspects of C# code.

Casing

There are several forms of casing used in .NET code.

Pascal Case

Pascal case capitalizes the first letter of each word. No spaces, underscores, or other characters separate the words.

```
✔   public class GregorianCalendar
    {
        // omitted
    }
```

In Pascal case, capitalize acronyms of two letters or fewer.

```
✔   public sealed class DBNull
    {
        // omitted
    }

✔   public enum GCCollectionMode
    {
        // omitted
    }
```

Camel Case

Camel case capitalizes the first letter of each word except the first word, which starts with a lower case letter. If there is only one word, render it in all lower case. In camel case, the humps are in the middle. Use camel case for a field, variable, or parameter that is not exposed outside the scope in which it is defined.

```
✔   private int gregorianCalendar;
```

In camel case, render acronyms at the beginning of the name in lowercase. In most cases, use acronyms only for very commonly understood concepts in the domain that the programmer is working in. For example, in an application dealing with databases, using the acronym "db" for a value from a database might be appropriate:

```
✔   private int dbValue;
```

Upper Case

Upper case capitalizes all letters. Use this for constants that come from other environments, such as the Windows API where capitalization is normally used. Also, use upper case for conditional compilation symbols. Use underscores to separate words.

```
✔ // From the Windows API
  private const int DATETIMES_SIZE = 132;

✔ #if DEBUG
      // omitted
  #endif
```

Code Contracts

Code Contracts are a Microsoft Research developed technology that can prove that code correctly implements contract rules specified in the code. They require considerable work to incorporate into the code, but can find many subtle bugs. They are a recommended, but optional, part of these best practices. Using Code Contracts should be adopted on a project-by-project basis. However, retroactively implementing Code Contracts is much more difficult than implementing them at the time of writing the code. Changing directions later will have considerable more cost than implementing them from the start.

Find Code Contracts for .NET online in the Extensions and Updates dialog. After installation, modify the settings in the Project Properties.

Rules that apply only if Code Contracts are used are marked with [Code Contracts] in the description.

Find more information about Code Contracts at http:// research.microsoft.com/en-us/projects/contracts

Copyright Notices

Copyright notices appear in several places in a project. In particular, they will appear in the file header for each file, as well as in the AssemblyCopyright attribute. They may also appear in the About dialog, help file, at the bottom of web pages, and other places in the application.

The suggested form is "Copyright © 2020 Acme Corporation"; however, consult with legal representation for the exact form that should be used in the country of publication. In the United States, (c) is not a substitution for a © symbol.

```
✔ [assembly: AssemblyCopyright("Copyright © 2020 Acme Corporation")]
```

All assemblies should have a copyright notice. Even free software should be assigned a copyright notice. It can then be released under a liberal license agreement.

Find more information about copyright notices in the *Circular 3: Copyright Notice* from the United States Copyright Office, http://www.copyright.gov/circs/circ03.pdf.

Typing Special Characters

There are several places where a rule requires a special character, such as ©, which is not on the normal keyboard. Windows provides an application called CharMap that allows typing these characters. To run CharMap, type ⊞+R, then type CharMap and press Enter. From there, select the wanted character, copy it to the clipboard, and then paste it into the source code.

Alternately, if the decimal numeric code for © is 169, then on most keyboards typing ALT+0169 will enter the character on the screen. That is, hold down the Alt key, then type 0169 on the numeric keypad, then release the Alt key. These are a few of the more common characters used in strings and comments that are not on the standard keyboard:

Symbol	Keystroke
™	ALT+0153
©	ALT+0169
®	ALT+0174
°	ALT+0176

Company Name

Throughout this book, the term "company" or "company name" can refer to other organizations that may not be traditional companies: *Miskatonic University* or the *Duchy of Grand Fenwick State Department* are a couple of examples. The term "company" is used throughout this book to mean the organization sponsoring writing the .NET application, regardless of its actual legal form. The AssemblyCompany attribute would be set to "Miskatonic University", if that were the sponsoring organization.

For the examples throughout this book, the company name used is the fictitious company *Acme Corporation*. This name is not related to any real company by any similar name. Acme Corporation is known as a fine supplier of a variety of equipment to a member of the species *canis latrans* for hunting *geococcyx californianus*. In a few other examples, *ACI* is the common acronym in use for *Acme Corporation International*, the fictitious parent company for Acme Corporation.

Frequently, the company name needs to be shortened for use in an identifier. Produce the shorter company name using a part of the name, or using an acronym. For example, Microsoft Corporation uses just "Microsoft" in identifier names. International Business Machines Corporation might use "IBM". Acme Corporation shortens the name to "Acme". The name used for company identifiers should be consistent across all .NET code produced within the company.

Internationalization

The Microsoft .NET platform has many features that make it relatively easy to internationalize a program or web site. The amount of work it takes to prepare an application for internationalization (I18N) is much less when writing an application than trying to retrofit it later. Planning should be in place for translating a program up front, even if the initial release of the program is in only one language.

Just doing the work to anticipate internationalizing a program causes it to be structured better, regardless of whether it is ever translated. For example, inserting all strings into resource files is a better place to manage them than hard coding them into the source code. In the resource files, an editor can review the strings in one place for spelling and grammar problems, catching them before the application ships.

A little tip: for the first translation to another language, try translating the resource strings into Pig Latin. Microsoft internally uses this as a testing tool to make sure that all interface items that should be translated actually are translated. Automated tools can perform the translation from English to Pig Latin.

Logging Errors

Logging packages makes easy recording information such as an unexpected exception. Some logging libraries for .NET are NLog, Log4net, and the Microsoft Enterprise Library. Logging unexpected exceptions is especially recommended. Logging can also be used for debugging in environments where installing an interactive debugger would be difficult, such as a web server or a client machine.

Version Control System

All code should be maintained by a version control system. The Visual Studio 2015 supports Microsoft Team Foundation Server (TFS), and Git when installed, and can support other systems such as Subversion through extensions. Code should be checked in periodically, and release builds should only be created from checked in code.

There are services that will act as hosts for the version control if maintaining an internal server is too difficult, for example VisualStudio.com and GitHub.com.

Code does not need comments indicating who wrote the code. Retrieve that information from the version control system.

Readability, Maintainability, and Performance

Try to write the code in such a way that it is easy to read and maintain. There may be a choice between writing easy to read and maintain code, and more "clever" code. In such cases, the preference should be for the easy to read and maintain code.

Only in cases where performance is critical should the weighting to change to allow more obscure code, if necessary. Even in a performance critical application, most code is not performance critical. If the code is obscure for performance reasons, additional comments are necessary to document what the code is doing.

On the other hand, when there are two ways to write code that are equally readable, but one has better performance, write it to perform better. Consider this code:

```
✗   for (int item = 0; item < PerformanceTest.Limit; item++)
    {
        // omitted
    }
```

Each iteration of the while loop retrieves the PerformanceTest.Limit property. Assuming that this property has a constant value for the duration of the loop (it should!), it can be placed into a local variable before the loop, and the local variable used. This saves the cost of retrieving the property on each iteration of the loop. The readability is about the same, but the performance is better.

```
✓   int limit = PerformanceTest.Limit;
    for (int item = 0; item < limit; item++)
    {
        // omitted
    }
```

With an IDE (Integrated Development Environment) such as Visual Studio, tab completion makes typing long names just as fast as typing short names. In cases where tab completion is not available, use Code Snippets in Visual

Studio to speed up typing. Remember that the code is written only once. Reading the code happens many times.

Some programmers act as if there is a tax for each character they add to an identifier name and use cryptic short names. Code written by such programmers is difficult to read and maintain. In .NET, words should be spelled out.

```
✗  int cnxSrv1;

✓  int connectionToServer1;
```

Breaking Changes and Compatibility

When modifying the code of a library after the first release of the code, it is important to be aware of the impact of making a change on compatibility between the calling code and the new library code. This is particularly true of libraries placed into the global assembly cache because they are shared. The kinds of compatibility are:

- Binary compatibility

- API compatibility

- Source code compatibility

A binary compatible change in a library is one that does not require any change in the component that calls on it. This typically happens when the implementation of the code in the library changes without changes to the public signature. Any change that is not binary compatible with the previous version is considered a "breaking change".

An API level compatible change in a library is one where a recompile of the component that calls it will cause the component to continue to work, with no change to the source code. An example is changing the return value of a method to a subclass of the type that it originally returned. Although this is a breaking change at the binary level, it requires no changes to the source code, and recompiling the source code that uses the method will cause the code to continue to work.

Any other change in a library is one that breaks source code compatibility. This means that a change will be necessary in the source code of the calling component to be able to use the new version of the library.

In general, binary compatible changes can be made without affecting the calling code. API and source code compatible changes will require some serious thought about the impact they make. If there is only one client of a library, and the library and the client are released together, then these changes will have little impact. However, if there are multiple clients released on different schedules, the impact of the change can be considerable. API and source code compatible changes are usually prohibited in a widely used library.

CODING CONVENTIONS

The coding conventions that follow are alphabetically organized. In some cases, the conventions refer to other sections that are a more general classification. Sometimes there will be two sections: one for defining something, and another for using the thing that is defined.

Arrays

These related sections also apply to arrays:

- Identifiers
- Scope

✴ Arrays **should** be jagged rather than multi-dimensional.

A jagged array is actually an array of arrays. Each of the secondary arrays can be of different lengths. In some implementations of a multi-dimensional array, some elements may not be filled with data. In such cases, a jagged array is preferred.

⊗ If all of the array cells will be filled with useful information, and all the dimensions will have the same number of elements, then a multi-dimensional array may be the best choice and the Code Analysis warning can be suppressed.

```
✗  public int[,] someField;
✓  public int[][] someField;
```

▶ Code Analysis CA1814

Assemblies

An assembly is both the logical concept of a package of executable code, as well as the physical file that contains that package. This section addresses both concepts.

✴ An assembly name **must** use Pascal case.

```
✗  Acme.exampleAssembly
✓  Acme.ExampleAssembly
```

▸ Code Analysis CA1709, StyleCop SA1300

✳ An assembly **should** have only one top-level namespace.

An assembly should have only one top-level namespace. It can have as many sub-namespaces of that top-level namespace as necessary.

```
✗ Acme.Finance.dll contains these namespaces:
  Acme.Finance
  Acme.GlobalResources
  Acme.Manufacturing

✓ Acme.Finance.dll contains these namespaces:
  Acme.Finance
  Acme.Finance.Accounting
  Acme.Finance.Planning
  Acme.Finance.Projecting
  Acme.Finance.Spending
```

✳ An assembly **should** have a namespace with the name of the assembly in it.

If an assembly is named Acme.Globalization.dll, then it should contain the namespace Acme.Globalization, and possibly sub-namespaces of that, and no other namespaces.

```
✗ Acme.Globalization.dll contains these namespaces:
  Acme.Formatter
  Acme.ObscureDateParser

✓ Acme.Globalization.dll contains these namespaces:
  Acme.Globalization
  Acme.Globalization.Formatter
```

✳ An assembly name **should** use the pattern: CompanyName. ComponentName.dll or CompanyName.ComponentName. SubComponentNames.dll (or exe).

The assembly name should have the parts separated by periods. The company name should be the first part of the assembly name of a component (possibly shortened, see the section on Company Name). The second part is the name of the component that the assembly represents. This may be further broken down with subcomponent names.

```
✓  Acme.PortableHole.dll

✓  Acme.PortableHole.Windows.dll

✓  Acme.PortableHole.Windows.resources.dll

✓  Acme.PortableHole.Generator.dll

✓  Acme.PortableHole.Generator.exe
```

⊗ Some projects are developed as a group collaborative project instead of by a company. Typically, these are open-source projects, managed on GitHub or CodePlex. If there is no sponsoring company or organization, then name the assembly using the pattern ProjectName.dll (or exe).

```
✓  StyleCop.dll
```

✳ An assembly **must** be signed with a strong name.

A strong name provides a unique identifier for a particular compilation of an assembly. A strong name includes the simple text name of the assembly, the version number, optional culture information, a digital signature, and the public key that corresponds to the private key used for signing. Two assemblies with the same strong name will be identical.

Visual Studio or the sn.exe command line tool can produce the keys necessary to produce a strong name.

A strong name is required to insert an assembly into the Global Assembly Cache.

An assembly that has strong name can only reference other assemblies with strong names. Assemblies with strong names can live side by side in the Global Assembly Cache with other versions of the same assembly. Assemblies in the Global Assembly Cache will be Just-In-Time compiled only once.

The strong name uses Public Key Encryption. If the private key is kept secure, then this guarantees that there is no tampering with a referenced assembly with a given public key. Although by itself this is does not guarantee security of applications, it is one component of a security scheme.

The strong name is specified in the Signing tab of the Project Properties in Visual Studio.

⊗ There may be cases where a reference is needed to a required library has not been given a strong name, and there is no way of adding one.

There is no other solution than not signing the assembly. If possible, though, work on acquiring a version of the library that has a strong name.

► Code Analysis CA2210

Assembly Attributes

The AssemblyInfo.cs file contains attributes that describe the assembly. These are placed into the metadata for the assembly, and are read by Windows and install programs. Microsoft has been casual about describing what should go into each of these attribute, and inconsistent on their use in their own assemblies. This section gives a consistent treatment on what should go into each one.

The Windows File Explorer will allow checking of many of the attributes of a file. Right click on the file and select Properties from the menu. The Details tab will show the value of many of the attributes.

This is a typical AssemblyInfo.cs file:

```
// ----------------------------------------------------------------
// <copyright file="AssemblyInfo.cs" company="Acme Corporation">
// Copyright © 2020 Acme Corporation
// </copyright>
// <summary>Implements the assembly attributes</summary>
// ----------------------------------------------------------------
using System;
using System.Diagnostics.Contracts;
using System.Reflection;
using System.Resources;
using System.Runtime.InteropServices;

[assembly: AssemblyCompany("Acme Corporation")]
#if DEBUG
[assembly: AssemblyConfiguration("Debug")]
#else
[assembly: AssemblyConfiguration("Release")]
#endif
[assembly: AssemblyCopyright("Copyright © 2020 Acme Corporation")]
[assembly: AssemblyDelaySign(false)]
[assembly: AssemblyDescription("Generates a portable hole.")]
[assembly: AssemblyInformationalVersion("1.0")]
[assembly: AssemblyProduct("Acme.PortableHole")]
[assembly: AssemblyTitle("Acme Portable Hole Library")]
[assembly: AssemblyTrademark(
    "Acme is a trademark of Acme Corporation")]
[assembly: AssemblyVersion("1.0.*")]
[assembly: CLSCompliant(true)]
[assembly: ComVisible(false)]
[assembly: ContractVerification(true)]
[assembly: Guid("E7A74D4E-9903-4181-ABFF-260E2CC5FCC5")]
[assembly: NeutralResourcesLanguage("en-US")]

/// <summary>Gives information about the assembly.</summary>
internal static class AssemblyInfo
{
    /// <summary>Gets an assembly attribute.</summary>
    /// <typeparam name="T">Assembly attribute type.</typeparam>
    /// <returns>The assembly attribute of type T.</returns>
    internal static T Attribute<T>() where T : Attribute
    {
        return
            typeof(AssemblyInfo).Assembly.GetCustomAttribute<T>();
```

```
        }
    }
```

There are times where an assembly attribute will need to be retrieved from the code. For example, a copyright notice may need to be placed inside an About dialog or at the bottom of a web page. The copyright notice should be retrieved from the AssemblyCopyright attribute.

In the code given above, there is the class AssemblyInfo that is added to the bottom of the AssemblyInfo.cs file. Using this class, assembly attributes can be retrieved. For example, this code will retrieve two of the attributes:

```
✓  string company =
        AssemblyInfo.Attribute<AssemblyCompanyAttribute>().Company;
   string copyright =

   AssemblyInfo.Attribute<AssemblyCopyrightAttribute>().Copyright;
```

Note that the code will throw a NullReferenceException if the attribute does not exist. If it is possible that the attribute will not exist, then the attribute will have to be checked for null before retrieving the property.

```
✓  string company = null;
   AssemblyCompanyAttribute companyAttribute =
        AssemblyInfo.Attribute<AssemblyCompanyAttribute>();
   if (companyAttribute != null)
   {
        company = companyAttribute.Company;
   }
```

In C# version 6, the code can be modified to allow for missing attributes with the null conditional operator.

```
✓  // Only works in C# version 6
   string company =
        AssemblyInfo.Attribute<AssemblyCompanyAttribute>()?.Company;
```

The code examples for retrieving the attributes in this section assume that the attribute is always present and use the C# version 5 syntax.

✱ All assembly attributes **should** be placed into the AssemblyInfo.cs file, stored in the Properties directory located in the root of the project.

> The Visual Studio project templates will create this file; however, it will need to be modified to include the necessary attributes.

⊗ There are a few exceptions to this rule. Attributes such as TypeForwardedTo and SuppressMessage may appear in other files. Assembly SuppressMessage attributes usually appear in the GlobalSuppressions.cs file.

✳ AssemblyCompany: The AssemblyCompany attribute **must** have the legal name of the company or organization that developed the assembly.

The Application.UserAppDataPath and Application.UserAppDataRegistry properties use the company name to create the directory and registry keys where information is stored.

```
✓ [assembly: AssemblyCompany("Acme Corporation")]

✓ // To retrieve the value
  string company =
      AssemblyInfo.Attribute<AssemblyCompanyAttribute>().Company;
```

✳ AssemblyConfiguration: The AssemblyConfiguration attribute **must** specify the configuration that was used to build the assembly.

Use conditional compilation to include different assembly configurations. Check for a conditional compilation symbol defined for this compilation and include the appropriate AssemblyConfiguration attribute.

```
✓ #if DEBUG
  [assembly: AssemblyConfiguration("Debug")]
  #else
  [assembly: AssemblyConfiguration("Release")]
  #endif

✓ // To retrieve the value
  string configuration =
      AssemblyInfo.Attribute<AssemblyConfigurationAttribute>()
      .Configuration;
```

If the project contains additional configurations besides Debug and Release, define a new conditional compilation symbol for the configuration in the Visual Studio project properties, and then add an #elif clause for the new configuration.

```
✔ #if DEBUG
  [assembly: AssemblyConfiguration("Debug")]
  #elif EXTENSIVE_LOGGING
  [assembly: AssemblyConfiguration("Extensive Logging")]
  #else
  [assembly: AssemblyConfiguration("Release")]
  #endif
```

✳ AssemblyCopyright: The AssemblyCopyright attribute **must** have the copyright notice for the assembly.

See the section on Copyright Notices for more information on the notice itself.

```
✔ [assembly: AssemblyCopyright("Copyright © 2020 Acme Corporation")]

✔ // To retrieve the value
  string copyright =
      AssemblyInfo.Attribute<AssemblyCopyrightAttribute>()
      .Copyright;
```

To print the copyright symbol in a console application, set the console output encoding to UTF8.

```
✔ Console.OutputEncoding = Encoding.UTF8;
  Console.WriteLine(copyright);
```

✳ AssemblyCulture: The AssemblyCulture attribute **may** be omitted.

The AssemblyCulture attribute is used to indicate the culture used for the assembly. For all but satellite assemblies, it must be designated with a zero length string. Because the only value likely to be used is an empty string, it may be omitted, which accomplishes the same result.

The compiler consumes this attribute and does not place it into the intermediate language. Therefore, the value cannot be retrieved.

```
✔ // This attribute may be omitted
  [assembly: AssemblyCulture("")]
```

✻ AssemblyDefaultAlias: The AssemblyDefaultAlias attribute **may** contain a friendly name for the assembly.

The AssemblyDefaultAlias attribute provides an alternate friendly name for the assembly when the assembly file name is something unfriendly, such as a randomly generated name. Since a randomly generated name would not follow the best practice for assembly names, it would be highly unusual to need an AssemblyDefaultAlias attribute, and it is infrequently used.

```
✓ // Rarely used
   [assembly: AssemblyDefaultAlias("Generated Assembly")]

✓ // To retrieve the value
   string defaultAlias =
       AssemblyInfo.Attribute<AssemblyDefaultAliasAttribute>()
       .DefaultAlias;
```

✻ AssemblyDelaySign: The AssemblyDelaySign attribute **must** contain a Boolean value indicating whether to delay sign the assembly.

If delay signing is needed, set the value to true, otherwise set it to false. Delayed signing is used when the author of the assembly does not have access to the private key that will be used eventually to sign the assembly. In most cases, a private key only used for development should be used instead of delay signing, and the release private key substituted when the product is shipped.

```
✓ // Used in most cases
   [assembly: AssemblyDelaySign(false)]

✓ // Rarely used
   [assembly: AssemblyDelaySign(true)]

✓ // To retrieve the value
   bool delaySign =
       AssemblyInfo.Attribute<AssemblyDelaySignAttribute>()
       .DelaySign;
```

✳ AssemblyDescription: The **AssemblyDescription** attribute **must** contain a short description of the purpose of this assembly.

This attribute provides a description of the purpose of this library. This should be a one-sentence or sentence fragment description, ending in a period.

```
✔ // The Acme.StockRetrieverLibrary project has this attribute
  [assembly: AssemblyDescription(
      "Retrieves stock information from a web service.")]

✔ // To retrieve the value
  string description =
      AssemblyInfo.Attribute<AssemblyDescriptionAttribute>()
      .Description;
```

✳ AssemblyFileVersion: The **AssemblyFileVersion** attribute **may** be set to the version number of the specific file of the assembly.

The AssemblyFileVersion attribute is used as the version number of the specific file, as opposed to the version number of the assembly. This version number is used as the Win32 file version in the assembly, which is shown in the Windows interface, as well as used by some programs that read that value. This number cannot contain a wildcard to generate build and revision numbers, unlike the AssemblyVersion attribute.

If the AssemblyFileVersion attribute is not present, then the AssemblyVersion attribute is used. Using the AssemblyVersion for the file version is usually correct, so in most cases this attribute should not be present.

```
✔ // Rarely used
  [assembly: AssemblyFileVersion("1.0.0.0")]

✔ // To retrieve the value
  string fileVersion =
      AssemblyInfo.Attribute<AssemblyFileVersionAttribute>()
      .Version;
```

✳ AssemblyInformationalVersion: The AssemblyInformationalVersion attribute **should** be set to the major and minor version number of the product.

The Application.UserAppDataPath or Application.UserAppDataRegistry properties reference paths and registry keys by building a string from the AssemblyCompany, AssemblyProduct, and AssemblyInformationalVersion attributes. If this attribute is not present, then the value in AssemblyVersion attribute is used instead. If the wildcard is used in the AssemblyVersion attribute, the compiler will change the build and revision number on each build causing information stored on the disk and registry to be stored in a different directory or registry key.

The AssemblyInformationalVersion attribute is used to provide a consistent version number for this version of the product. It should be changed along with the AssemblyVersion attribute number when the major or minor version is changed.

```
✔ [assembly: AssemblyInformationalVersion("3.0")]
  [assembly: AssemblyVersion("3.0.*")]

✔ string informationalVersion = AssemblyInfo
      .Attribute<AssemblyInformationalVersionAttribute>()
      .InformationalVersion;
```

⊗ Under some rare circumstances, the AssemblyInformationalVersion attribute might be set to some other value than a pure version number. For example, suppose that there was a special build for a particular customer that should use separate registry keys or file paths. In such cases, it can be set to an arbitrary string. However, using an arbitrary string will cause a Code Analysis warning that can be suppressed. In such a case the attribute might be set like this:

```
✔ // Rarely used
  [assembly: AssemblyInformationalVersion("3.0 CustomerX Build")]
```

✳ AssemblyProduct: The AssemblyProduct attribute **must** contain the product name of the product of which this assembly is a part.

The product is the deliverable to the customer. In this example, Acme Financial Analysis and Acme Portfolio Analyzer are separate products.

```
✔  // The Acme.FinancialAnalysis project has this attribute
   [assembly: AssemblyProduct("Acme.FinancialAnalysis")]

✔  // The Acme.PortfolioAnalyzer project has this attribute
   [assembly: AssemblyProduct("Acme.PortfolioAnalyzer")]
```

The Acme Stock Retriever Library is only used and delivered with the Portfolio Analyzer. Therefore, the product for the Stock Retriever is the Portfolio Analyzer.

```
✔  // The Acme.StockRetrieverLibrary project has this attribute
   [assembly: AssemblyProduct("Acme.PortfolioAnalyzer")]
```

The Acme Business Library however is used by multiple projects or is delivered on a different schedule than the code that uses it. In this case, the product is the library itself.

```
✔  // The Acme.BusinessLibrary project has this attribute
   [assembly: AssemblyProduct("Acme.BusinessLibrary")]
```

To retrieve the value:

```
✔  string product =
        AssemblyInfo.Attribute<AssemblyProductAttribute>().Product;
```

✱ AssemblyTitle: The AssemblyTitle attribute **must** contain the friendly name for this assembly.

The AssemblyTitle is the friendly name of this particular assembly describing what it does. A friendly name can contain spaces and other punctuation. Use this attribute to populate the name of the program in About dialogs and anywhere else the name of the program is given for human consumption.

```
✔  // The Acme.FinancialAnalysis project has this attribute
   [assembly: AssemblyTitle("Acme Financial Analysis")]

✔  // To retrieve the value
   string title =
        AssemblyInfo.Attribute<AssemblyTitleAttribute>().Title;
```

✱ AssemblyTrademark: The **AssemblyTrademark** attribute **should** be included if any trademarks or service marks are asserted in the assembly.

Trademarks should be stated in complete sentences with a period at the end. Consult with legal representation for the exact wording of such statements. If no trademarks or service marks are asserted, then this attribute can be omitted.

```
✓ [assembly: AssemblyTrademark(
       "Acme is a trademark of Acme Corporation.")]

✓ // To retrieve the value
  string trademark =
      AssemblyInfo.Attribute<AssemblyTrademarkAttribute>()
      .Trademark;
```

✱ AssemblyVersion: The **AssemblyVersion** attribute **must** contain a valid version number for the assembly.

The version number is constructed from four values:

- Major Version
- Minor Version
- Build Number
- Revision

Applications run only with versions of a library for which they were built, by default. It is important to have the version marked. Versions are considered the same if the major and minor versions are the same.

For initial releases, the major and minor version numbers should be set to 1.0. Major and minor releases should increment these numbers by one. When the major version is incremented, the minor version should be reset to zero.

On an executable, the major and minor version numbers should change depending on how much new functionality has been added. Major amount of new functionality increment the major version number. Minor amounts of new functionality increment the minor version number.

On a library, the major version number should be incremented by one when the library is not binary compatible with the previous version of the library. The minor version number should be incremented by one when new features are added that do not break binary compatibility with the previous version. A bug fix or testing release would use the current major and minor numbers with the automatically generated build and revision numbers.

The build and revision numbers are numbers that change for each build of the assembly. In most cases, the build and release numbers should be specified as an asterisk, which lets the compiler maintain them. If an asterisk is used, the build number will increment daily. The revision number is generated from the current time on the Windows clock, so should be larger on each build. If there are more than one computer that is used to provide released builds it is important that they all have their computer clocks synchronized with each other, and that the time zones specified for the computers be identical.

There may be pathological cases where a new build has a lower build and revision number than a previous build, such as two separate builds on different computers where one computer's clock is not set correctly. Another is a build at the point the clock is reset in the fall when Daylight Saving Time ends. Deliveries of assemblies should have the version number checked before being released to a customer to verify that it always increases.

The AssemblyVersion is not a normal attribute. The compiler performs special operations on its value, and does not write the AssemblyVersion information into an attribute in the intermediate language, so it cannot be retrieved in the same way as other assembly attributes.

```
✗ [assembly: AssemblyVersion("0.9.*")]

✗ [assembly: AssemblyVersion("1.0.3.27")]

✓ [assembly: AssemblyVersion("1.0.*")]

✓ // To retrieve the value, assuming AssemblyInfo is a class in
   // the assembly
   Version version = typeof(AssemblyInfo).Assembly.GetName().Version;
```

When the major or minor version numbers are changed, the AssemblyInformationalVersion attribute should also be changed.

▸ Code Analysis CA1016

✱ CLSCompliant: The **CLSCompliant** attribute **must** be present and indicate the CLS compliance of the assembly.

```
✓ [assembly: CLSCompliant(true)]
```

```
✔ [assembly: CLSCompliant(false)]

✔ // To retrieve the value
  bool clsCompliant =
      AssemblyInfo.Attribute<CLSCompliantAttribute>().IsCompliant;
```

▸ Code Analysis CA1014

✳ ComVisible: The ComVisible attribute **must** be present and indicate the default visibility to COM.

In most cases, the value for the ComVisible attribute for the assembly should be false. Apply the ComVisible attribute with the true value to the specific components that needs to be visible.

```
✔ [assembly: ComVisible(false)]

✔ // Rarely used
  [assembly: ComVisible(true)]

✔ // To retrieve the value
  bool comVisible =
      AssemblyInfo.Attribute<ComVisibleAttribute>().Value;
```

▸ Code Analysis CA1017

✳ [Code Contracts] ContractVerification: The ContractVerification attribute **must** be passed a Boolean value indicating the default static contract verification.

The value passed to the ContractVerification attribute becomes the default state for static analysis of the assembly. If the value passed is true, then static analysis is performed on the whole assembly, except where overridden. If the value passed is false, then no static analysis is performed, unless specifically overridden on a given class or member.

In most cases, the value should be set to true so that contracts are verified for the entire assembly. However if contracts are being added to an existing assembly there may be hundreds or thousands of warnings. In such case, the default can be set to false, and then turned on for a specific class or method to limit the number of warnings to a manageable level while they are handled. After they are handled, the assembly value can be set back to true.

```
✔ [assembly: ContractVerification(true)]
```

```
✓ [assembly: ContractVerification(false)]
```

This attribute is consumed by the Code Contracts component and not actually written to the intermediate language. It, therefore, cannot be retrieved.

✳ Guid: The Guid attribute **must** be present and assigned to a unique value.

The Guid attribute uniquely identifies this assembly to COM. The value must not be copied from any other assembly; it should be generated by a Guid generator. A Guid generator can be found in Visual Studio on the Tools menu. The Guid attribute places a universally unique number into the assembly that can be retrieved by reflection.

```
✓ [assembly: Guid("518dfb74-78ea-46dd-a4ac-3bda80e47290")]

✓ // To retrieve the value
  string guid = AssemblyInfo.Attribute<GuidAttribute>().Value;
```

✳ InternalsVisibleTo: The InternalsVisibleTo attribute **may** be included to expose internal variables to other libraries.

This attribute allows access to the internals of an assembly to another assembly. The most common use of this attribute is to expose the internals of this assembly to a unit test assembly. If the assembly is properly signed with a strong name, then the PublicKey property needs to be the public key of the strong name of the assembly specified.

```
✓ [assembly: InternalsVisibleTo(
      "Acme.BusinessLibrary.Tests, PublicKey="
    + "00230000048000009400000006020000002400005253413100040000001"
    + "000100af8c79272a210350b3bee38fc437d529342ff61c2bf0067a5bf2"
    + "afc4a5fb6882004440c4887769b52e5fce97a90504671375c4041cc67e"
    + "b70c3458ac1ff711725b2ff19f1c923fed44890a49be4499acb88f5f42"
    + "375ed6f1415172f1ed23b5783ec01ce3df747f2b035ba0e306d205311c"
    + "de0ec620da77455ef6bef8309450b2")]

✓ // To retrieve a single value
  string internalsVisibleTo =
      AssemblyInfo.Attribute<InternalsVisibleToAttribute>()
      .AssemblyName;
```

There can be more than one InternalsVisibleTo attribute in the assembly to allow access to different assemblies. In such case, the

AssemblyInfo.Attribute method will not work, and it will throw an AmbiguousMatchException. Retrieving the values at runtime then requires code that is slightly more complicated.

```
✔ // To retrieve a collection of values
  IEnumerable<InternalsVisibleToAttribute> allInternals =
      typeof(AssemblyInfo).Assembly.
      GetCustomAttributes<InternalsVisibleToAttribute>();
  foreach (InternalsVisibleToAttribute internals in allInternals)
  {
      string internalsVisibleTo = internals.AssemblyName;

      // omitted
  }
```

✷ NeutralResourcesLanguages: The NeutralResourcesLanguages in an assembly **must** be set to the language of the resources contained within it.

If an assembly contains resources, the NeutralResourcesLanguages attribute identifies that the assembly shares the language neutral resources and the language specified in the attribute. This makes it clear to .NET that it does not need to look for a satellite assembly for that language. In most cases, the value specified will be the codes for the language and country of the programming team, and the default language of the user interface. This value is set to the RFC 1766 (https://tools.ietf.org/html/rfc1766) specifier for the language and country of the neutral resources.

Even if the assembly does not have any resources, the attribute indicates the language and country of the comments specified by the developers.

```
✔ [assembly: NeutralResourcesLanguageAttribute("en-US")]

✔ string neutralResourcesLanguage =
      AssemblyInfo.Attribute<NeutralResourcesLanguageAttribute>()
      .CultureName;
```

- Code Analysis CA1824

Attributes (Defining a New Custom Attribute)

These related sections also apply to defining a new custom attribute:

- Classes**Error! Reference source not found.**
- Identifiers
- Scope
- Types

✳ A custom attribute definition class name **must** be defined using Pascal case.

```
✗   internal sealed class someAttribute : Attribute
    {
        // omitted
    }
✓   internal sealed class SomeAttribute : Attribute
    {
        // omitted
    }
```

▶ Code Analysis CA1709, StyleCop SA1300

✳ A custom attribute definition class name **must** be suffixed by the word **Attribute**.

```
✗   internal sealed class ContractAbbreviator : Attribute
    {
        // omitted
    }
✓   internal sealed class ContractAbbreviatorAttribute : Attribute
    {
        // omitted
    }
```

▶ Code Analysis CA1710

✳ A custom attribute definition class **must** be sealed.

A method that accesses a custom attribute must traverse the inheritance hierarchy unless the class is sealed. A sealed custom attribute definition provides better performance.

```
✗  internal class SomeAttribute : Attribute
   {
       // omitted
   }
✓  internal sealed class SomeAttribute : Attribute
   {
       // omitted
   }
```

▸ Code Analysis CA1813

✳ A custom attribute definition class **must** be decorated with an AttributeUsage attribute specifying where it can be used.

The AttributeUsage attribute specifies where the custom attribute can be used.

```
✗  internal sealed class SomeAttribute : Attribute
   {
       // omitted
   }
✓  [AttributeUsage(AttributeTargets.All)]
   internal sealed class SomeAttribute : Attribute
   {
       // omitted
   }
```

▸ Code Analysis CA1018

✳ Each mandatory argument to the constructor for an attribute **must** have a read-only property that retrieves the value.

```
✗  [AttributeUsage(AttributeTargets.All)]
   public sealed class SomeAttribute : Attribute
   {
       private string item;
```

```
        public SomeAttribute(string item)
        {
            this.item = item;
        }
    }
✓   [AttributeUsage(AttributeTargets.All)]
    public sealed class SomeAttribute : Attribute
    {
        private string item;

        public SomeAttribute(string item)
        {
            this.item = item;
        }

        public string Item
        {
            get
            {
                return this.item;
            }
        }
    }
```

▶ Code Analysis CA1019

Attributes (Using an Attribute)

✳ An attribute **must** be placed on the line above the element that it decorates, and indented to the level of the element.

Place multiple attributes on successive lines.

```
✗   [Pure]public int SomeMethod()
    {
        // omitted
    }
✓   [Pure]
    public int SomeMethod()
    {
```

```
        // omitted
    }

✔  [DebuggerStepThrough]
    [Pure]
    public int SomeMethod()
    {
        // omitted
    }
```

✱ Multiple attributes **must** be listed in alphabetical order.

This makes it easier to check if several similar methods are all decorated the same way.

```
✘  [Pure]
    [DebuggerStepThrough]
    public int SomeMethod()
    {
        // omitted
    }

✔  [DebuggerStepThrough]
    [Pure]
    public int SomeMethod()
    {
        // omitted
    }
```

✱ An attribute **must** be the only element on a line.

This includes other attributes. This makes it easier to see which attributes are specified.

```
✘  [DebuggerStepThrough][Pure]
    public int SomeMethod()
    {
        // omitted
    }

✔  [DebuggerStepThrough]
    [Pure]
    public int SomeMethod()
    {
```

```
        // omitted
    }
```

＊ An attribute must be individually surrounded by square brackets.

An attribute must be individually surrounded by square brackets, not part of a comma-separated list of attributes. Lists of attributes are harder to read.

```
✗  [DebuggerStepThrough, Pure]
   public int SomeMethod()
   {
       // omitted
   }
✓  [DebuggerStepThrough]
   [Pure]
   public int SomeMethod()
   {
       // omitted
   }
```

＊ An attribute must not be suffixed by the word Attribute when used.

This provides a consistent way of referring to attributes.

```
✗  [PureAttribute]
   public int SomeMethod()
   {
       // omitted
   }
✓  [Pure]
   public int SomeMethod()
   {
       // omitted
   }
```

✳ An attribute constructor without arguments **must not** be followed by parentheses.

If the argument list for the constructor is empty, then the parentheses should be omitted. This provides a consistent way of referring to attributes.

```
✗  [Pure()]
   public int SomeMethod()
   {
       // omitted
   }

✓  [Pure]
   public int SomeMethod()
   {
       // omitted
   }
```

▶ StyleCop SA1411

✳ An attribute that has a URL, GUID, or Version argument or property **must** be passed a valid value.

In a normal class, a URL, GUID, or Version argument or property would be assigned to the result of calling the constructor of the appropriate data type. However, the processing of attribute happens at compile time, and thus can only contain constants, so these must be represented by strings. The string for a URL, GUID, or version must have the correct format for the data type that it represents.

```
✗  [SomeAttribute(Guid = "NotAGUID")]
   public class SomeClass
   {
       // omitted
   }

✓  [SomeAttribute(Guid = "B53E77F6-1959-4B9E-9B66-F76C6AB7734A")]
   public class SomeClass
   {
       // omitted
   }
```

▶ Code Analysis CA2243

✴ An **Obsolete** attribute constructor **must** be passed a message argument.

The message should describe some reason why the item is now obsolete.

```
✗ [Obsolete]
  public class SomeClass
  {
      // omitted
  }

✓ [Obsolete("Will be removed in the next release.")]
  public class SomeClass
  {
      // omitted
  }
```

▶ Code Analysis CA1041

Classes

These related sections also apply to classes:

- Identifiers
- Scope
- Types

✴ A class name **must** use Pascal case.

```
✗ public class someClass
  {
      // omitted
  }

✓ public class SomeClass
  {
      // omitted
  }
```

▶ Code Analysis CA1709, StyleCop SA1300

✴ A class name **must not** be named the same as a namespace in the project.

For example, if there is a Helper namespace in the assembly, do not name a class Helper as well.

✴ A class name **should** be a noun or noun phrase.

Classes generally represent a kind of object, and therefore a noun. The class name should reflect that.

```
✗   public class ConnectToWebServer
    {
        // omitted
    }

✓   public class WebServer
    {
        // omitted
    }
```

✴ A class name **must not** be prefixed.

Do not prefix class names with a C. Some naming conventions, particularly in C++, prefix all class names with a C.

```
✗   public class CSomeClass
    {
        // omitted
    }

✓   public class SomeClass
    {
        // omitted
    }
```

▶ Code Analysis CA1722

✴ A class name **must not** include an underscore character.

Use Pascal case, not underscores, to separate words.

```
✗   public class Some_Class
    {
        // omitted
    }
```

```
✓  public class SomeClass
   {
       // omitted
   }
```

✴ A class name **may** begin with the letter I.

The class name is distinguished from a similar interface by the capitalization, as an interface will start with two capital letters.

```
✓  /// <summary>Class to test if something is red.</summary>
   public class IfRed
   {
       // omitted
   }
✓  /// <summary>Interface for Fred.</summary>
   public interface IFred
   {
       // omitted
   }
```

✴ A class that only contains static members **should** be marked static.

```
✗  public class SomeClass
   {
       public static void SomeMethod()
       {
           // omitted
       }
   }
✓  public static class SomeClass
   {
       public static void SomeMethod()
       {
           // omitted
       }
   }
```

▶ Code Analysis CA1053

✷ An internal or private class that is never instantiated **must** be removed.

An internal or private class that is never instantiated is unused. Remove or comment out this code.

▸ Code Analysis CA1812

✷ A class that contains extension methods that extend another class **must** be named with the name of the class being extended suffixed with **Extensions**.

This makes it easy to find the extensions methods for a class.

```
✗ public static class SomeClass
  {
      public static Rectangle Corners(this Bitmap bitmap)
      {
          // omitted
      }
  }
✓ public static class BitmapExtensions
  {
      public static Rectangle Corners(this Bitmap bitmap)
      {
          // omitted
      }
  }
```

✷ An abstract class **must not** have a constructor.

Constructors on abstract types can be called only by derived types. Because public constructors create instances of a type, and instances of abstract types cannot be created, an abstract type that has a public constructor is incorrectly designed.

```
✗ public abstract class SomeClass
  {
      public SomeClass()
      {
          // omitted
      }
  }
```

```
✓ public abstract class SomeClass
   {
       // omitted
   }
```

▶ Code Analysis CA1012

✳ Inheritance **should not** be excessively deep.

A general rule of thumb is that an inheritance hierarchy should not be more than four levels deeper than the base class.

```
✗ public class SomeClass
   {
       // omitted
   }

   public class SomeClassDerived1 : SomeClass
   {
       // omitted
   }

   public class SomeClassDerived2 : SomeClassDerived1
   {
       // omitted
   }

   public class SomeClassDerived3 : SomeClassDerived2
   {
       // omitted
   }

   public class SomeClassDerived4 : SomeClassDerived3
   {
       // omitted
   }

   public class SomeClassDerived5 : SomeClassDerived4
   {
       // omitted
   }
```

▶ Code Analysis CA1501

✳ A class **must not** inherit from certain other classes.

Do not inherit from any of the following classes:

- ApplicationException
- CollectionBase
- DictionaryBase
- Queue
- ReadOnlyCollectionBase
- SortedList
- Stack
- XmlDocument

Inherit from Exception or one of its subclasses in the System namespace, not ApplicationException. When a class has a generic and non-generic version, inherit from the generic version of a class. For example, inherit from SortedList<int> instead of SortedList.

```
✗   public class SomeList : SortedList
    {
        // omitted
    }

✓   public class SomeList : SortedList<int>
    {
        // omitted
    }

✗   public class SomeException : ApplicationException
    {
        // omitted
    }

✓   public class SomeException : Exception
    {
        // omitted
    }
```

▶ Code Analysis CA1058

Code (General Rules)

✴ Goto statements **should** be used when the alternatives are harder to understand.

Edgar Djikstra wrote a famous paper in 1968, *GO TO Statement Considered Harmful* that laid out the case for why goto statements should be avoided: They generally make hard to follow code. At the time, languages such as Basic and FORTRAN required frequent use of goto statements, which, when used incorrectly, led to spaghetti code. With the advent of structured programming languages, the constructs in the language frequently make most goto statements unnecessary. However, the original reason for avoiding goto statements is sometimes lost, which is to make the code clear.

Consider these two examples:

```
✗   public void SomeMethod(int exitValue)
    {
        bool exitLoops = false;
        for (int i = 1; i < 10; i++)
        {
            for (int j = 1; j < 10; j++)
            {
                if (i * j == exitValue)
                {
                    exitLoops = true;
                    break;
                }

                // omitted
            }

            if (exitLoops)
            {
                break;
            }
        }
    }
✓   public void SomeMethod(int exitValue)
    {
        for (int i = 1; i < 10; i++)
        {
```

```
            for (int j = 1; j < 10; j++)
            {
                if (i * j == exitValue)
                {
                    goto ExitLoops;
                }

                // omitted
            }
        }

ExitLoops:
    }
```

The first example is much harder to understand than is the second. It also runs slightly slower because frequent tests on the exitLoops Boolean variable. The second example is much preferred. Exiting nested loops is one of the primary reasons that a goto statement should be used, as the alternatives in C# are always more convoluted. However, there are other cases where a goto statement will make the code easier to read.

Some programming teams might require a code review before allowing a goto statement.

✳ Strings **should** be normalized to upper case.

Normalize strings to upper case, particularly before performing a case insensitive comparison.

```
✗  string value1 = "Some Words";
   string value2 = value1.ToLower(CultureInfo.InvariantCulture);
✓  string value1 = "Some Words";
   string value2 = value1.ToUpper(CultureInfo.InvariantCulture);
```

In some international strings, normalizing to lower case produces different results than normalizing to upper case. Here is one small example of code that produces different results. In Unicode (http://www.unicode.org), code point 03F1 is the symbol "ϱ", which is a Greek Rho. The code point 03C1 is the symbol "ρ", which is the small Greek Rho symbol. Both of these are Rho, so should compare. When upper cased, both turn into the code point 03A1, which is the capital Greek Rho, and has the symbol "Ρ". Lower casing the capital Greek Rho returns the small Greek Rho. This code demonstrates what happens:

```
✓  string greekRho = "\u03f1";
   string greekRhoSmall = "\u03c1";

   // This writes "True"
   Console.WriteLine(greekRho.ToUpper() == greekRhoSmall.ToUpper());

   // This writes "False"
   Console.WriteLine(greekRho.ToLower() == greekRhoSmall.ToLower());

   // This writes "False"
   Console.WriteLine(greekRho.ToUpper().ToLower() == greekRho);

   // This writes "True"
   Console.WriteLine(
       greekRhoSmall.ToUpper().ToLower() == greekRhoSmall);
```

▶ Code Analysis CA1308

✳ A test for an empty string **must not** compare to "" or string.Empty.

Do not test for empty strings by comparing them to "" or string.Empty. Instead check to see if the string.Length property is zero, or use string.IsNullOrEmpty or string.IsNullOrWhiteSpace.

```
✗  if (input != null && input != string.Empty)
   {
       // omitted
   }
✓  if (input != null && input.Length != 0)
   {
       // omitted
   }
✓  if (!string.IsNullOrEmpty(input))
   {
       // omitted
   }
```

▶ Code Analysis CA1820

✳ Strings **should** use ordinal for comparisons.

Pass the StringComparison.Ordinal or
StringComparison.OrdinalIgnoreCase enum value, when comparing two
non-linguistic strings.

```
✗   string name1 = @"c:\temp\file1";
    string name2 = @"c:\temp\file2";

    if (string.Equals(name1, name2,
    StringComparison.InvariantCulture))
    {
        // omitted
    }
✓   string name1 = @"c:\temp\file1";
    string name2 = @"c:\temp\file2";

    if (string.Equals(name1, name2, StringComparison.Ordinal))
    {
        // omitted
    }
```

▸   Code Analysis CA1309

✳ The **Debug.Assert** method **must** be passed the message text
argument.

The message argument should give a text description of what is being
asserted.

```
✗   Debug.Assert(value != null);
✓   Debug.Assert(value != null, "value must not be null");
```

▸   StyleCop SA1405

✳ The **Debug.Fail** method **must** be passed the message text
argument.

```
✗   Debug.Fail(string.Empty);
✓   Debug.Fail("This code should never be reached");
```

▸   StyleCop SA1406

✳ Casts **should not** be performed multiple times if it can be avoided.

Casts have a performance cost. If possible, only perform a cast once. When performing a cast, the as operator can frequently be used, then the result checked for null.

In the following example, the is operator performs a cast to check if the object is a string, then the actual cast is performed. In the preferred code, this is replaced by using an as operator and a check for null.

```
✗  public static void SomeMethod(object item)
   {
       if (item is string)
       {
           string thing = (string)item;

           // omitted code that uses "thing"
       }
   }
✓  public static void SomeMethod(object item)
   {
       string thing = item as string;
       if (thing != null)
       {
           // omitted code that uses "thing"
       }
   }
```

▶ Code Analysis CA1800

✳ Arithmetic expressions **must** declare precedence.

Arithmetic expressions must use parentheses to indicate the order of evaluation. The implicit rules of evaluation should not be used. This makes it clear what the programmer intended.

```
✗  int value = 4 * input + 3;
✓  int value = (4 * input) + 3;
```

▶ StyleCop SA1407

✷ Conditional expressions **must** declare precedence.

Conditional expressions must use parentheses to indicate the order of evaluation. The implicit rules of evaluation should not be used. This makes it clear what the programmer intended.

```
✘  if (x == 4 || y == 5 && z == 7 || w == 9)
   {
       // omitted
   }

✔  if ((x == 4 || y == 5) && (z == 7 || w == 9))
   {
       // omitted
   }
```

▶ StyleCop SA1408

✷ Unnecessary parentheses **should** be removed.

Parentheses that are not required by the C# syntax and do not give any additional information to the programmer about the order of evaluation must be removed.

```
✘  int value = (input + 2);

✔  int value = input + 2;
```

▶ StyleCop SA1119

✷ Code **must** use the C# alias for types, not the .NET Framework type.

In the table below, the C# type alias must always be used, not the type or fully qualified type.

✓ C# Type Alias	✗ Type	✗ Fully Qualified Type
bool	Boolean	System.Boolean
byte	Byte	System.Byte
char	Char	System.Char
decimal	Decimal	System.Decimal
double	Double	System.Double
float	Single	System.Single
int	Int32	System.Int32
long	Int64	System.Int64
object	Object	System.Object
sbyte	SByte	System.SByte
short	Int16	System.Int16
string	String	System.String
uint	UInt32	System.UInt32
ulong	UInt64	System.UInt64
ushort	UInt16	System.UInt16

```
✗  using System;
   // omitted
   private String value = String.Empty;

✗  private System.String value = string.Empty;

✓  private string value = string.Empty;
```

The most frequent violation of this rule is to use **String** instead of **string** to declare a string variable. The lower case **string** is a C# type alias, whereas the upper case **String** is a class that is defined in the System namespace and requires a **using** statement for the System namespace to be declared before it can be used.

▶ StyleCop SA1121

✱ The var keyword **should not** be used, except in very limited circumstances.

The code is easier to read and understand when declarations use an explicit data type, particularly when reading code outside of Visual Studio.

```
✗  var count = 10;

✓  int count = 10;
```

There are a few circumstances where the var keyword should be used. In a LINQ query declarations, the var keyword is preferred.

```
✗  var cityList = new string[]
        {
            "Seattle",
            "Vancouver",
            "Portland",
            "Spokane"
        };

   IEnumerable<string> cities =
       from city in cityList
       where city[0] == 'S'
       select city;

   foreach (var city in cities)
   {
       // omitted
   }

✓  string[] cityList =
       { "Seattle", "Vancouver", "Portland", "Spokane" };
   var cities =
       from city in cityList
       where city[0] == 'S'
       select city;

   foreach (string city in cities)
   {
       // omitted
   }
```

Notice, however, that the declaration of cityList and the declaration of city in the foreach statement are both declared with string and not var.

There are some situations where the var keyword is required. In these cases, the data type is an anonymous type known only to the compiler.

```
✓  Customer[] customerList =
   {
       new Customer("Attel Malagate", "555-0100", "Medina"),
```

```
        new Customer("Kokor Hekkus", "555-0101", "Mercer Island"),
        new Customer("Hagbard Celine", "555-0102", "Seattle")
    };

    var customers =
        from customer in customerList
        where customer.City == "Seattle"
        select new
        {
            customer.Name,
            customer.Phone
        };

    foreach (var item in customers)
    {
        Console.WriteLine(
            "Name={0}, Phone={1}", item.Name, item.Phone);
    }
```

In the example above, the var keyword is required in the declaration in the foreach statement because the data type is anonymous and only known to the compiler.

✱ Unnecessary code **should** be removed.

Code that could be removed without changing the overall logic should be removed.

In the example below, both the try and catch blocks are empty. This code should be removed.

```
✗ try
    {
    }
    catch (Exception ex)
    {
    }
```

In the example below, the try block has code, but there are no catch blocks and the finally block is empty. The try-finally can be removed, although the call to the method should be preserved.

```
✗ try
    {
        this.SomeMethod();
    }
```

```
finally
{
}
```

In the example below, the **unsafe** statement is empty. It can be removed.

```
✗ unsafe
  {
  }
```

- ▶ StyleCop SA1409

✳ Empty finalizers **must** be removed.

A finalizer that has no content must be removed. If an object has an empty finalizer, it will be called during one garbage collection, but the object will not be removed until the next garbage collection. This hurts performance.

```
✗ public class SomeClass
  {
      // omitted

      ~SomeClass()
      {
      }

      // omitted
  }
✓ public class SomeClass
  {
      // omitted
  }
```

- ▶ Code Analysis CA1821

✳ Special folder names **must** be retrieved from Environment.GetFolderPath.

Strings that represent special folders in Windows, such as the Program Files directory, must not be hard coded. Instead, they should be retrieved from the Environment.GetFolderPath method using the Environment.SpecialFolder enum. These locations are in different locations in different versions of Windows, and the locations are localized.

```
✗   string path = @"\Program Files (x86)";

✓   string path = Environment.GetFolderPath(
        Environment.SpecialFolder.ProgramFilesX86);
```

This is a list of the values of the Environment.SpecialFolder enum in the .NET Framework 4.0: AdminTools, ApplicationData, CDBurning, CommonAdminTools, CommonApplicationData, CommonDesktopDirectory, CommonDocuments, CommonMusic, CommonOemLinks, CommonPictures, CommonProgramFiles, CommonProgramFilesX86, CommonPrograms, CommonStartMenu, CommonStartup, CommonTemplates, CommonVideos, Cookies, Desktop, DesktopDirectory, Favorites, Fonts, History, InternetCache, LocalApplicationData, LocalizedResources, MyComputer, MyDocuments, MyMusic, MyPictures, MyVideos, NetworkShortcuts, Personal, PrinterShortcuts, ProgramFiles, ProgramFilesX86, Programs, Recent, Resources, SendTo, StartMenu, Startup, System, SystemX86, Templates, UserProfile, Windows.

See the documentation for the Environment.SpecialFolder enum for the complete description of these values and the folders to which they refer.

▶   Code Analysis CA1302

Collections (defining a new collection)

These related sections also apply to defining a new collection:

- Classes

- Identifiers

- Scope

- Types

✱ A class that defines a collection **should** end in the suffix Collection, or a more specific suffix.

Pick the suffix from the following table:

Base Type or Interface	Suffix
DataSet	DataSet or Collection
DataTable	DataTable or Collection
ICollection	Collection
IDictionary	Dictionary
IEnumerable	Collection
Queue	Queue or Collection
Stack	Stack or Collection

```
✗   public class Buffer : Queue
    {
        // omitted
    }

✓   public class BufferQueue : Queue
    {
        // omitted
    }
```

▶ Code Analysis CA1710

✳ Lists **should** be strongly typed.

When creating a new list type, the collection should be strongly typed.
Do not just create a class that just inherits from IList, which is weakly
typed.

```
✗   public class SomeCollection : IList
    {
        // omitted
    }
```

Instead, inherit from **CollectionBase**, and implement IList<T>. Then add
whatever additional functionality is necessary to the class. The code
below shows a basic implementation.

```
✓   public class SomeCollection<T> : CollectionBase, IList<T>
    {
        public bool IsReadOnly
        {
            get
            {
```

```
            return this.List.IsReadOnly;
        }
    }

    public T this[int index]
    {
        get
        {
                return (T)this.List[index];
        }

        set
        {
            this.List[index] = value;
        }
    }

    public void Add(T item)
    {
        this.List.Add(item);
    }

    public bool Contains(T item)
    {
        return this.List.Contains(item);
    }

    public void CopyTo(T[] array, int arrayIndex)
    {
        this.List.CopyTo(array, arrayIndex);
    }

    public int IndexOf(T item)
    {
        return this.List.IndexOf(item);
    }

    public void Insert(int index, T item)
    {
        this.List.Insert(index, item);
    }

    public new IEnumerator<T> GetEnumerator()
    {
```

```
        return (IEnumerator<T>)base.GetEnumerator();
    }

    public bool Remove(T item)
    {
        int count = this.Count;
        this.List.Remove(item);
        return this.Count != count;
    }
}
```

▶ Code Analysis CA1039

Comments

XMLComments have a separate section.

✳ A comment **should** impart information that the code itself does not.

A comment should impart information that is not directly in the code, such as its intention, the implementation of an algorithm, information about the real world thing the code is trying to represent, or other information for the programmer who must maintain the code. A comment that adds no additional information over what a competent programmer reading the code would understand is of no value and should be removed.

For example, suppose that there is this code:

```
✗   public void SomeMethod()
    {
        int someField = 1;

        // omitted

        // This code multiplies someField by 2
        someField *= 3;

        // omitted
    }
```

The comment says that someField is multiplied by 2; however, the code multiplies it by 3. Obviously there is a problem, but which is wrong, the comment or the code? More than likely, someone has changed the code without changing the comment. Even if it matched the code, the comment imparts no information that a reading of the code would not give. In this case, just omitting the comment would be correct. If the comment is omitted, the code may still be wrong and should be multiplying by 2; however, the programmer does not need to spend time understanding both the code and the comment before fixing the code. Changing the comment to explain why the field is being multiplied would also be correct.

```
✓ public void SomeMethod()
  {
      int someField = 1;

      // omitted

      someField *= 3;

      // omitted
  }
✓ public void SomeMethod()
  {
      int someField = 1;

      // omitted

      // Allow for extra space on each side of what someField
      // allocates so we can insert stuff before and after it.
      someField *= 3;

      // omitted
  }
```

✳ A comment **must** be indented to the level of the statement it is commenting.

Comments should be indented to the same level as the code that they are describing.

```
✗ // Defines the value of the Golden Ratio
     double phi = (1 + Math.Sqrt(5)) / 2;

✓        // Defines the value of the Golden Ratio
         double phi = (1 + Math.Sqrt(5)) / 2;
```

✱ A comment **must** be preceded with a blank line, unless starting a block or continuing another comment.

A blank line above a comment opens up the code and makes it easier to read. A comment at the start of a block, however, should not have a blank line above it.

```
✗  // Defines the ratio of the circumference
   // of a circle to its radius.
   double tau = Math.PI * 2;
   // Defines the value of the Golden Ratio.
   double phi = (1 + Math.Sqrt(5)) / 2;

✓  // Defines the ratio of the circumference
   // of a circle to its radius.
   double tau = Math.PI * 2;

   // Defines the value of the Golden Ratio.
   double phi = (1 + Math.Sqrt(5)) / 2;

✓  public void SomeMethod()
   {
       // Defines the ratio of the circumference
       // of a circle to its radius.
       double tau = Math.PI * 2;

       // omitted
   }
```

▸ StyleCop SA1515

✱ A comment **should not** be followed by a blank line.

Attach a comment to the code that follows it by not having any blank lines between the comment and the following code.

```
✗  // Defines the value of the Golden Ratio.

   double phi = (1 + Math.Sqrt(5)) / 2;

✓  // Defines the value of the Golden Ratio.
   double phi = (1 + Math.Sqrt(5)) / 2;
```

▸ StyleCop SA1512

✳ A comment **must not** be specified using delimited comments (/* */).

Use the // comment specifier, not the delimited comment specifier. This makes comments consistent throughout the code.

```
✗   /* Defines the value of the Golden Ratio. */
    double phi = (1 + Math.Sqrt(5)) / 2;

✓   // Defines the value of the Golden Ratio.
    double phi = (1 + Math.Sqrt(5)) / 2;
```

✳ A comment **must not** be placed on lines with other code.

A comment should appear before the code it describes.

```
✗   double phi = (1 + Math.Sqrt(5)) / 2; // The Golden Ratio.

✓   // The Golden Ratio.
    double phi = (1 + Math.Sqrt(5)) / 2;
```

✳ A comment **must** not be empty.

Comments should have content. An empty comment should be removed or replaced by a blank line.

```
✗   //
    // Checks argument
    //
    if (arg == 3)
    {
        // omitted
    }

✓   // Checks argument
    if (arg == 3)
    {
        // omitted
    }
```

  ▸ StyleCop SA1120

✳ A single-line comment **must** begin with a single space.

Comments must begin with a single space. This makes the comment easier to read and differentiates it from removed code.

```
✗  //Some comment.

✓  // Some comment.
```

- ▸ StyleCop SA1005

✳ A comment that temporarily removes code **must** use ////.

A comment that temporarily removes code must use four slashes. These do not need to be followed by a space. This helps delineate code that is temporarily removed from normal single-line comments.

These should be reviewed periodically and removed if the code is no longer needed.

```
✗  //double phi = (1 + Math.Sqrt(5)) / 2;

✓  ////double phi = (1 + Math.Sqrt(5)) / 2;
```

✳ Single line comments within the code **must not** use ///.

Three slashes are used for XML comments, and should not be used for single line comments.

```
✗  /// Defines the value of the Golden Ratio.
   double phi = (1 + Math.Sqrt(5)) / 2;

✓  // Defines the value of the Golden Ratio.
   double phi = (1 + Math.Sqrt(5)) / 2;
```

- ▸ StyleCop SA1626

✳ A comment **must not** come between a block statement definition and the opening curly brace of the block.

Place the comment inside the block, not before it.

```
✗  if (value == 1)
       // Causes failure
   {
       // omitted
   }

✓  if (value == 1)
   {
       // Causes failure
```

```
    // omitted
}
```

▸ StyleCop SA1108

Constants

These related sections also apply to constants:

- Identifiers
- Scope

✳ A constant field **must** use Pascal case.

```
✗ private const double phi = 1.618033988749;

✓ private const double Phi = 1.618033988749;
```

▸ Code Analysis CA1709, StyleCop SA1300, SA1303

✳ A local constant **must** use camel case.

```
✗ public void SomeMethod()
  {
      const double Phi = 1.618033988749;

      // omitted
  }
✓ public void SomeMethod()
  {
      const double phi = 1.618033988749;

      // omitted
  }
```

✳ A constant **must** be defined on a line by itself.

Lines with multiple declarations are harder to read.

```
✗ private const double Phi = 1.618033988749, Pi = 3.14159265358979;

✓ private const double Phi = 1.618033988749;
  private const double Pi = 3.14159265358979;
```

✳ A constant **should** be used for something that is computable at compile time.

A constant value is computed at compile time, whereas a static readonly field is computed at run time. Uses of a constant are replaced with the value at compile time, whereas a static readonly field remains a reference. There is a performance cost to using a static readonly field.

⊗ Use a public constant only for something that will never change, since changing the value is a breaking change to any client code that uses the constant.

```
✗ private static readonly int Item = 6;

✓ private const int Item = 6;
```

▶ Code Analysis CA1802

✳ A public constant **should** only be defined for something that will never change, even between versions of the program.

Because a constant name is replaced by the compiler with its value in the Intermediate Language, a change of the value of a public constant is a breaking change. Use a static readonly variable for something that might change between versions, so that changes of the value are not breaking.

Code Analysis rule CA1802 may need to be suppressed.

```
✗ public readonly static double Phi = 1.618033988749;
  public const string Version = "Program version 3.9";

✓ public const double Phi = 1.618033988749;
  public static readonly string Version = "Program version 3.9";
```

Constructors

✳ If there are a series of overloaded constructors, they **should** all directly call the most complex constructor.

If there are a series of overloaded constructors that take an increasing number of arguments, they should each directly call the most complex of the constructors, rather than calling one of the other less complex constructors. This makes it so each of the constructors, except the most complex one, is independent of the other constructors and can be individually removed or changed without rewriting more code than is necessary.

```
✗   public class SomeClass
    {
        private int count;
        private DateTime dateCreated;
        private string name;

        public SomeClass ()
            : this(string.Empty)
        {
        }

        public SomeClass (string name)
            : this(name, 0)
        {
        }

        public SomeClass (string name, int count)
            : this(name, count, DateTime.Now)
        {
        }

        public SomeClass(
            string name,
            int count,
            DateTime dateCreated)
        {
            this.name = name;
            this.count = count;
            this.dateCreated = dateCreated;
        }
    }

✓   public class SomeClass
    {
        private int count;
        private DateTime dateCreated;
        private string name;

        public SomeClass()
            : this(string.Empty, 0, DateTime.Now)
        {
        }
```

```
    public SomeClass(string name)
        : this(name, 0, DateTime.Now)
    {
    }

    public SomeClass(string name, int count)
        : this(name, count, DateTime.Now)
    {
    }

    public SomeClass(string name, int count, DateTime dateCreated)
    {
        this.name = name;
        this.count = count;
        this.dateCreated = dateCreated;
    }
}
```

✸ A static constructor **should** be used when the order of execution of static field initializers is important.

The C# specification says that the order of execution of the initializers of static fields is the order they appear in the code. If code is refactored, the order can change, causing hard to track down bugs. If one static field is dependent on another static field, their initialization should be moved to a static constructor, where the order of initialization is explicit.

Code Analysis warning CA1810 recommending that the code be moved back to the static initializers may need to be suppressed.

```
✗ public class Rocket
  {
      private static Widget widget = new Widget();
      private static Gadget gadget = widget.Sprocket;
  }

✓ public class Rocket
  {
      private static Gadget gadget;
      private static Widget widget;

      [SuppressMessage("Microsoft.Performance",
          "CA1810:InitializeReferenceTypeStaticFieldsInline",
          Justification = "Initialization order matters.")]
```

```
        static Rocket()
        {
            widget = new Widget();
            gadget = widget.Sprocket;
        }
    }
```

Contracts

✳ [Code Contracts] Contracts **must** use the specified ordering.

The order of Contracts:

1. If-then-throw. Backward-compatible public preconditions.

2. Requires, Requires<E>. All public preconditions.

3. Ensures. All public (normal) postconditions.

4. EnsuresOnThrow. All public exceptional postconditions.

5. Ensures. All private/internal (normal) postconditions.

6. EnsuresOnThrow. All private/internal exceptional postconditions.

7. EndContractBlock. If using if-then-throw-style preconditions without any other contracts, place a call to EndContractBlock to indicate that all previous "if" checks are preconditions.

Controls

✳ A control that does not need to be named **should** be left unnamed.

In WPF, Silverlight, and other XAML based technologies, not every control needs to be named. In general, a control only needs to be named if it is accessed in code or a storyboard. A control such as a TextBlock frequently does not need to be named if the content never changes and the control is not referenced in code.

✳ A control name **must** be prefixed with the data type of the control.

For example, if a control is a close button, the name should be ButtonClose. When treading this code, this helps to know what kind of control is being referenced.

```
✗   <Button x:Name="Close"
        Width="75"
        Height="23"
        Content="Close"
        IsCancel="True"
        IsDefault="True" />

✓   <Button x:Name="ButtonClose"
        Width="75"
        Height="23"
        Content="Close"
        IsCancel="True"
        IsDefault="True" />
```

✳ In XAML based technologies, controls **should** be named
with the x:Name attribute, not the Name attribute.

The Name attribute is a string field of the FrameworkElement class that
most controls inherit from, whereas the x:Name attribute is defined by
XAML itself. The Name attribute is mapped to the x:Name attribute by
the RuntimeNameProperty attribute. Because x:Name applies to all XAML
elements and Name does not, x:Name is preferred.

```
✗   <Button Name="ButtonClose"
        Width="75"
        Height="23"
        Content="Close"
        IsCancel="True"
        IsDefault="True" />

✓   <Button x:Name="ButtonClose"
        Width="75"
        Height="23"
        Content="Close"
        IsCancel="True"
        IsDefault="True" />
```

Delegates

These related sections also apply to delegates:

- Identifiers
- Scope
- Types

✳ Delegate parentheses **must** be removed when an anonymous delegate has no parameters.

```
✗ this.SomeMethod(delegate()
  {
      return 1;
  });

✓ this.SomeMethod(delegate
  {
      return 1;
  });
```

▸ StyleCop SA1410

Enums

These related sections also apply to enums:

- Identifiers
- Scope
- Types

Enums are used two separate ways: as a set of separate values, or as a set of flags. Flags are noted by using the Flags attribute. Flags allow the bitwise operators such as & and | to apply to the flags to construct values that are not necessarily one of the existing enum values. The rules are slightly different between flags and values enums.

As an example, a values enum of the days of the week would typically allow only one day of the week to be selected, whereas a flags enum of the days of the week would allow multiple days of the week to be selected. Flags enums are usually declared using powers of two, whereas value enums are usually just listed sequentially.

✳ An enum name **must** use Pascal case.

```
✗ public enum days
  {
      // omitted
  }

✓ public enum Days
  {
```

```
        // omitted
    }
```

▶ Code Analysis CA1709, StyleCop SA1300

✳ An enum name **must not** include a suffix.

In particular, do not end enums with Enum or Flags suffix.

```
✗  [Flags]
   public enum DaysFlags
   {
        // omitted
   }

✗  public enum DayEnum
   {
        // omitted
   }

✓  [Flags]
   public enum Days
   {
        // omitted
   }

✓  public enum Day
   {
        // omitted
   }
```

✳ An enum **should** be defined using the default Int32 data type.

Enums should be left to the default Int32 data type.

```
✗  public enum Day : short
   {
        // omitted
   }

✓  public enum Day
   {
        // omitted
   }
```

⊗ If the enum needed to represent values in a larger range than would fit into an Int32, it is permissible to use a long (Int64) data type.

```
✔ public enum BigNumber : long
  {
      MinValue = 0x0,
      MaxValue = &x0FFFFFFFFFFFF
  }
```

▶ Code Analysis CA1028

✳ A flags enum **must** be decorated with a **Flags** attribute.

```
✘ public enum Days
  {
      None = 0x00,
      Sunday = 0x01,
      Monday = 0x02,
      Tuesday = 0x04,
      Wednesday = 0x08,
      Thursday = 0x10,
      Friday = 0x20,
      Saturday = 0x40
  }
✔ [Flags]
  public enum Days
  {
      None = 0x00,
      Sunday = 0x01,
      Monday = 0x02,
      Tuesday = 0x04,
      Wednesday = 0x08,
      Thursday = 0x10,
      Friday = 0x20,
      Saturday = 0x40
  }
```

▶ Code Analysis CA1027

✳ A flags enum **should** be named with plural name.

```
✘ [Flags]
  public enum Day
  {
```

```
        None = 0x00,
        Sunday = 0x01,
        Monday = 0x02,
        Tuesday = 0x04,
        Wednesday = 0x08,
        Thursday = 0x10,
        Friday = 0x20,
        Saturday = 0x40
    }
✓  [Flags]
    public enum Days
    {
        None = 0x00,
        Sunday = 0x01,
        Monday = 0x02,
        Tuesday = 0x04,
        Wednesday = 0x08,
        Thursday = 0x10,
        Friday = 0x20,
        Saturday = 0x40
    }
```

With the Days enum defined in the example, other values could be constructed from combinations of values:

```
✓  Days weekend = Days.Saturday | Days.Sunday;
```

▸   Code Analysis CA1714

✳ A values enum **should** have a singular name.

In the example for Color, a variable can be set to only one of the colors in the Color enum.

```
✗  public enum Colors
    {
        Red,
        Green,
        Blue,
        Yellow,
        Cyan,
        Magenta
    }
```

```
✓  public enum Color
   {
       Red,
       Green,
       Blue,
       Yellow,
       Cyan,
       Magenta
   }
```

▶ Code Analysis CA1717

Enum Values

These related sections also apply to enum values:

- Identifiers

✱ An enum value **must** use Pascal case.

```
✗  public enum Color
   {
       red,
       green,
       blue
   }
✓  public enum Color
   {
       Red,
       Green,
       Blue
   }
```

▶ Code Analysis CA1709, StyleCop SA1300

✱ An enum value **must not** include the type name.

Do not include the type name into the individual enum values.

```
✗  public enum Color
   {
       ColorRed,
       ColorGreen,
```

```
        ColorBlue
    }
✔  public enum Color
    {
        Red,
        Green,
        Blue
    }
```

▸ Code Analysis CA1712

✳ In a value enum, there **should** be an enum value equal to zero.

When a variable of is declare as an enum data type, the default value of the variable is zero. There should be an enum value name that equates to this value. If there is no value that is appropriate, insert a new value and name it **None**.

The value for zero can be defined explicitly or implicitly. If no values are given explicitly in the code, then the first enum value will have the value zero.

```
✗  public enum Color
    {
        Red = 1,
        Green = 2,
        Blue = 3
    }
✔  public enum Color
    {
        Red,
        Green,
        Blue
    }
✔  public enum Color
    {
        Red = 0,
        Green = 10,
        Blue = 20
    }
```

```
✔  public enum Color
   {
       None = 0,
       Red = 10,
       Green = 20,
       Blue = 30
   }
```

▸ Code Analysis CA1008

✱ In a flags enum, there **should** be an enum value named None with the value equal to zero.

In bit fields, None is the way to specify that no bits are set.

```
✗  [Flags]
   public enum Days
   {
       Sunday = 0x01,
       Monday = 0x02,
       Tuesday = 0x04,
       Wednesday = 0x08,
       Thursday = 0x10,
       Friday = 0x20,
       Saturday = 0x40
   }
✔  [Flags]
   public enum Days
   {
       None = 0x00,
       Sunday = 0x01,
       Monday = 0x02,
       Tuesday = 0x04,
       Wednesday = 0x08,
       Thursday = 0x10,
       Friday = 0x20,
       Saturday = 0x40
   }
```

▸ Code Analysis CA1008

✳ A flags enum value **must** either be a power of two or a combination of other values.

```
✗ [Flags]
  public enum Days
  {
      None = 0x00,
      Sunday = 0x01,
      Monday = 0x02,
      Tuesday = 0x03,
      Wednesday = 0x04,
      Thursday = 0x05,
      Friday = 0x06,
      Saturday = 0x07
  }
✓ [Flags]
  public enum Days
  {
      None = 0x00,
      Sunday = 0x01,
      Monday = 0x02,
      Tuesday = 0x04,
      Wednesday = 0x08,
      Thursday = 0x10,
      Friday = 0x20,
      Saturday = 0x40,
      Weekend = Saturday | Sunday
  }
```

▶ Code Analysis CA2217

✳ An enum value **must not** be named Reserved.

A reserved value is one that is meant to be named later. Renaming an enum value is a breaking change, whereas adding a new value is not. Either name the reserved value correctly or remove it entirely.

```
✗ public enum Color
  {
      Red,
      Reserved,
      Blue
  }
```

```
✔  public enum Color
   {
       Red,
       Green,
       Blue
   }

✔  public enum Color
   {
       Red = 0,
       Blue = 2
   }
```

► Code Analysis CA1700

Event Arguments

These related sections also apply to Event Arguments:

- Classes
- Identifiers
- Scope
- Types

✳ An event argument class **must** always inherit from EventArgs, either directly or indirectly.

```
✗  public class SomeEventArgs
   {
       // omitted
   }

✔  public class SomeEventArgs : EventArgs
   {
       // omitted
   }

✔  public class SomeOtherEventArgs : EventArgs
   {
       // omitted
   }

   public class SomeEventArgs : SomeOtherEventArgs
```

```
    {
        // omitted
    }
```

❋ An event arguments class name **must** end with suffix
EventArgs.

Any class that inherits from EventArgs, either directly or indirectly,
must have the suffix EventArgs.

```
✗   public class Example : EventArgs
    {
        // omitted
    }
✓   public class ExampleEventArgs : EventArgs
    {
        // omitted
    }
```

▶ Code Analysis CA1710

Event Handlers

These related sections also apply to event handler delegates and event
handler variables:

- Identifiers

- Scope

The argument to an event handler is listed in the section for Event
Arguments.

There are four parts to an event handler:

- An optional event handler delegate declaration establishing the type.

- An event handler variable that establishes the queue.

- An "On" method that calls the event handler queue.

- One or more event handler methods that are called.

The first three are placed in the class that defines and calls the event
handler. The event handler methods are placed in the calling code.

In addition, there are two other things that must be done to invoke an event
handler:

- The calling code must add the event handler method to the event handler variable.

- The "On" procedure must be called when the event is to occur.

With the availability of the generic event handlers, event handler delegates should be used infrequently. They are mainly used in providing a type inside a library to be used outside the library.

Here is an example of a class that establishes two events named Triggering and Triggered. Calling SomeMethod causes both events to occur. The Triggering event can be cancelled, whereas the Triggered event cannot.

```
namespace EventHandlerExample
{
    using System;
    using System.ComponentModel;

    public class TestClass
    {
        public event EventHandler Triggered;

        public event EventHandler<CancelEventArgs> Triggering;

        public bool SomeMethod()
        {
            CancelEventArgs cancelEventArgs =
                new CancelEventArgs(true);
            this.OnTriggering(cancelEventArgs);
            if (!cancelEventArgs.Cancel)
            {
                this.OnTriggered();
            }

            return !cancelEventArgs.Cancel;
        }

        protected virtual void OnTriggered()
        {
            if (this.Triggered != null)
            {
                this.Triggered(this, EventArgs.Empty);
            }
        }

        protected virtual void OnTriggering(CancelEventArgs e)
```

```
        {
            if (this.Triggering != null)
            {
                this.Triggering(this, e);
            }
        }
    }
}
```

Below is a console application that uses the code above:

```
namespace EventHandlerExample
{
    using System;
    using System.ComponentModel;

    public static class Program
    {
        public static void Main(string[] args)
        {
            TestClass testClass = new TestClass();
            testClass.Triggering += Triggering;
            testClass.Triggered += Triggered;
            if (testClass.SomeMethod())
            {
                Console.WriteLine("Completed");
            }
            else
            {
                Console.WriteLine("Canceled");
            }
        }

        private static void Triggered(
            object sender,
            EventArgs e)
        {
            Console.WriteLine("Triggered");
        }

        private static void Triggering(
            object sender,
            CancelEventArgs e)
        {
            Console.WriteLine("Triggering");
```

```
            // Change this to true to cancel
            e.Cancel = false;
        }
    }
}
```

✳ An event handler delegate name **must** use Pascal case.

```
✗ public delegate void someEventHandler(
      object sender,
      EventArgs e);

✓ public delegate void SomeEventHandler(
      object sender,
      EventArgs e);
```

  ▶ Code Analysis CA1709, StyleCop SA1300

✳ An event handler variable name **must** use Pascal case.

```
✗ public event EventHandler<CancelEventArgs> someEvent;

✓ public event EventHandler<CancelEventArgs> SomeEvent;
```

  ▶ Code Analysis CA1709, StyleCop SA1300

✳ An event handler delegate name **must** always end in the suffix EventHandler.

```
✗ public delegate void SomeDelegate(
      object sender,
      EventArgs e);

✓ public delegate void SomeEventHandler(
      object sender,
      EventArgs e);
```

  ▶ Code Analysis CA1710

✳ **An event handler delegate must always have two arguments, sender and e.**

The sender argument must always be of type object even if it is possible to use a more specific data type. The second argument must be of the data type EventArgs or a class that inherits from EventArgs.

```
✗  public delegate void SomeEventHandler(
       Button sender,
       EventArgs e);

✗  public delegate void SomeEventHandler(EventArgs e);

✓  public delegate void SomeEventHandler(
       object sender,
       EventArgs e);
```

▶ Code Analysis CA1009

✳ **An event Handler delegate must return void.**

Any return values from an event handler should be returned as a property of the class that inherits from EventArgs.

```
✗  public delegate int SomeEventHandler(
       object sender,
       EventArgs e);

✓  public delegate void SomeEventHandler(
       object sender,
       EventArgs e);
```

▶ Code Analysis CA1009

✳ **An event hander variable name must be declared with the event keyword.**

The event keyword changes the variable name from a field to an event. The impact of this keyword is subtle. When the event keyword is present, it has several effects that are not present in a normal field:

- An event can be defined in an interface.

- The visibility of the = and () operators become private, so only the class in which they are defined can assign or invoke them.

- The add and remove methods can be used to redefine what the += and -= operators perform.

```
✗  public EventHandler Triggered;

✓  public event EventHandler Triggered;
```

✱ An event handler variable name **should** be named using verbs.

```
✗  public event EventHandler ButtonEvent;

✓  public event EventHandler ClickEvent;
```

✱ An event handler variable name **may** have the suffix Event.

An event hander variable may have the suffix Event. It may also have no suffix at all. However, it should never have the suffix EventHandler or Delegate. The EventHandler suffix is only used on event handler delegates, and the Delegate suffix is never used.

```
✗  public event EventHandler ClickEventHandler;

✓  public event EventHandler Click;

✓  public event EventHandler ClickEvent;
```

✱ Related event handler variables, where one can be canceled, **should** be suffixed with ing and ed gerunds.

Do not use Before and After prefixes to indicate the different events.

```
✗  public event EventHandler<CancelEventArgs> BeforeExit;
   public event EventHandler AfterExit;

✓  public event EventHandler<CancelEventArgs> Exiting;
   public event EventHandler Exited;
```

▸ Code Analysis CA1713

✱ An event handler variable **should** be defined using a generic declaration.

Do not declare a delegate for an event handler. Instead, use the EventHandler generic declaration. This enforces that the event handler has the correct form.

```
✗  public delegate void SomeEventHandler(object sender, EventArgs e);
   // omitted
   public event SomeEventHandler SomeEvent;

✓  public event EventHandler SomeEvent;

✓  public event EventHandler<CancelEventArgs> SomeEvent;
```

⊗ In a library, it is sometimes acceptable to declare a delegate for an event handler if it is public and meant to be used in a declaration in the code using the library.

▶ Code Analysis CA1003

✱ There **should** be a method that is prefixed with On followed by the event name for each event.

If the event handler generic type is EventArgs or the second argument to the delegate of the event handler is EventArgs, then the method must take no arguments. If the event handler generic type is a class that inherits from EventArgs or the second argument to the delegate of the event handler is a class that inherits from EventArgs, then the method must have a single parameter of that type, and the name of the argument should be e.

If the class the "On" method is defined in is not sealed, then the method should be declared with the protected virtual modifiers, so that the method could be overridden in a derived class. If the class is sealed, then the method should have the private modifier.

The method should only have a single argument e that passes the event arguments. It should instantiate the event argument, and call the event handler if it is not null. In instance methods, the first argument should be this. These examples are for instance event handlers:

```
✓  protected virtual void OnTriggered()
   {
       if (this.Triggered != null)
       {
           this.Triggered(this, EventArgs.Empty);
       }
   }

✓  protected virtual void OnTriggering(CancelEventArgs e)
   {
       if (this.Triggering != null)
       {
```

```
            this.Triggering(this, e);
        }
    }
```

Event handler variables can also be defined as static, in which case the "On" method should also be declared as static. When calling static event handler variables, the first argument should be passed as null since there is no object sending the event.

```
✔ private static void OnTriggered()
    {
        if (Triggered != null)
        {
            Triggered(null, EventArgs.Empty);
        }
    }
✔ private static void OnTriggering(CancelEventArgs e)
    {
        if (Triggering != null)
        {
            Triggering(null, e);
        }
    }
```

✳ **Event handler methods in the calling code should be suffixed by name of the event handler variable.**

The name of a method that is called by the event handler should be suffixed the name of the event handler variable. In many cases, the name will just be the name of the event handler variable.

```
✔ // All of the following examples assume that there is this
    // class definition.
    public class SomeClass
    {
        public event EventHandler SomeEvent;

        // omitted
    }
✘ // In the calling code that subscribes to the event
    private static SomeClass someClass;

    public void Setup()
```

```
    {
        this.someClass = new SomeClass();
        this.someClass.SomeEvent += SomethingElse;
    }

    public void SomethingElse()
    {
        // omitted
    }
```

✔
```
    // In the calling code that subscribes to the event
    private SomeClass someClass;

    public void Main()
    {
        this.someClass = new SomeClass();
        this.someClass.SomeEvent += SomeEvent;
    }

    public void SomeEvent()
    {
        // omitted
    }
```

✔
```
    // In the calling code that subscribes to the event
    private SomeClass someClass;

    public void Main()
    {
        this.someClass = new SomeClass();
        this.someClass.SomeEvent += ButtonSomeEvent;
    }

    public void ButtonEvent()
    {
        // omitted
    }
```

✱ If the event handler has **add** and **remove** accessors, the **add** accessor **must** come first.

```
✗ private EventHandler someEvent;

  public event EventHandler SomeEvent
```

```
    {
        remove
        {
            this.someEvent -= value;
        }

        add
        {
            this.someEvent += value;
        }
    }
✓   private EventHandler someEvent;

    public event EventHandler SomeEvent
    {
        add
        {
            this.someEvent += value;
        }

        remove
        {
            this.someEvent -= value;
        }
    }
```

▶ StyleCop SA1213

Exceptions (Defining a New Exception)

These related sections also apply to defining a new exception:

- Classes
- Identifiers
- Scope
- Types

✱ A defined exception name **must** use Pascal case.

```
✗ public class someException : Exception
  {
```

```
        // omitted
    }

✓  public class SomeException : Exception
    {
        // omitted
    }
```

- ▸ Code Analysis CA1709, StyleCop SA1300

✳ A defined exception name **must** always end in the suffix
Exception.

```
✗  public class SomeFailure : Exception
    {
        // omitted
    }

✓  public class SomeException : Exception
    {
        // omitted
    }
```

- ▸ Code Analysis CA1710

✳ A defined exception **must** always inherit from
System.Exception either directly or indirectly.

System.Exception will be accessed through a using System; statement at
the top of the code, so the code will just show inheriting from Exception.

```
✗  public class SomeException
    {
        // omitted
    }

✓  public class SomeException : Exception
    {
        // omitted
    }

✓  public class SomeOtherException : Exception
    {
        // omitted
    }
```

```
public class SomeException : SomeOtherException
{
    // omitted
}
```

✳ A defined exception **should** have the public access modifier.

Code that throws an exception may be caught outside the current assembly. In the calling code, if the exception is not public, then only the base class that the exception inherited can be used to process the exception, which usually will not provide enough information.

```
✗   internal class SomeException : Exception
    {
        // omitted
    }

✓   public class SomeException : Exception
    {
        // omitted
    }
```

▶ Code Analysis CA1064

✳ A defined exception **must** supply the standard set of constructors.

A newly defined exception must supply the at least four constructors. If the exception is named SomeException, the constructors have these profiles:

- public SomeException()

- public SomeException(string)

- public SomeException(string, Exception)

- protected or private SomeException(SerializationInfo, StreamingContext)

```
✓   [Serializable]
    public class SomeException : Exception
    {
        public SomeException()
        {
            // omitted
```

```
        }

        public SomeException(string message)
            : base(message)
        {
            // omitted
        }

        public SomeException(string message, Exception innerException)
            : base(message, innerException)
        {
            // omitted
        }

        protected SomeException(
            SerializationInfo info,
            StreamingContext context)
            : base(info, context)
        {
            // omitted
        }
    }
```

Exceptions (Using Exceptions)

✳ An exception **should** only be thrown when something is truly exceptional.

For example, if there is a method that searches a collection, the method should not throw an exception if it does not find an item in the collection. In most code, not finding an item in a collection is something that happens frequently in the normal course of processing. The method should return a special value such as false or null when it does not find the item.

However, if the method should always find the item in the collection, but does not, then it should throw an exception.

✳ An exception **should** always be thrown when something is truly exceptional.

If something is exceptional, throw an exception. Do not return a status value for something that should not happen in the normal course of events. The standard way of indicating an error in C# is to throw an exception.

✳ The most specific exception that applies should be thrown.

If the code can throw either ArgumentException or ArgumentOutOfRangeException, the ArgumentOutOfRangeException should be thrown because it is more specific.

```
✘  if (value >= 3)
   {
       throw new ArgumentException(
           "Value must be less than 3",
           "value");
   }

✔  if (value >= 3)
   {
       throw new ArgumentOutOfRangeException(
           "Value must be less than 3",
           "value");
   }
```

✳ The variable or parameter name e must not be used to store or pass an exception.

Event handlers use a standard parameter named e that is used for the event arguments. Code that processes exceptions with e cannot be pasted into these event handlers. Use the variable name ex instead. Be careful about using code from the .NET Framework help files without modification, as the examples frequently use e for the exception variable name.

```
✘  try
   {
       // omitted
   }
   catch (FileNotFoundException e)
   {
       // omitted
   }

✔  try
   {
       // omitted
```

```
    }
    catch (FileNotFoundException ex)
    {
        // omitted
    }
```

✳ The variable name for an exception **should** be ex.

The variable ex is the standard variable name for exception handling.

```
✗   try
    {
        // omitted
    }
    catch (FileNotFoundException e)
    {
        // omitted
    }
✓   try
    {
        // omitted
    }
    catch (FileNotFoundException ex)
    {
        // omitted
    }
```

✳ A variable name **must not** be used in an exception handler if the variable is not used.

C# allows exception handlers with no variable if the exception variable is not used.

```
✗   try
    {
        // omitted
    }
    catch (FileNotFoundException ex)
    {
        throw;
    }
✓   try
    {
```

91

```
        // omitted
    }
    catch (FileNotFoundException)
    {
        throw;
    }
✓ try
    {
        // omitted
    }
    catch (FileNotFoundException ex)
    {
        Console.WriteLine("File open failed {0}", ex.Message);
    }
```

✳ An exception handler **should not** handle general exceptions
unless re-thrown.

These are the general exceptions:

- catch (System.Exception)

- catch (System.SystemException)

- catch

Catching general exceptions tends to catch exceptions that should have
been anticipated and a more specific exception handled. A more specific
exception should be caught instead.

A general exception can be caught if it is re-thrown before exiting the
exception handler.

```
✗ try
    {
        // omitted
    }
    catch
    {
        // omitted
    }
✓ try
    {
        // omitted
    }
```

```
    catch
    {
        // omitted
        throw;
    }
✓  try
    {
        // omitted
    }
    catch (FileNotFoundException)
    {
        // omitted
    }
```

⊗ The entry point method in an executable may handle general exceptions, since this is the top of the call stack. Generally, an exception that reaches this exception handler is actually a bug where the exception should have been handled at a lower level in the call stack. In the exception handler, the exception should be reported to the user and logged in some way that programmers can review. After handling the general error, the program should return the program to a stable state if it can. If the program cannot be restored to a stable state, it may exit gracefully. Code Analysis warning CA1031 will need to be suppressed.

▶ Code Analysis CA1031

✳ Exceptions **should not** be thrown from unexpected locations.

Certain kinds of code should not throw exceptions. They are:

- Property Get Methods

- Event Accessor Methods

- Equals Methods

- GetHashCode Methods

- ToString Methods

- Static Constructors

- Finalizers

- Dispose Methods

- Equality Operators

- Implicit Cast Operators

All of these are expected to execute without throwing an exception. Refactor the code so it does not throw an exception.

```
✗  private int someProperty = 1;

   public int SomeProperty
   {
       get
       {
           if (this.someProperty > 3)
           {
               throw new InvalidOperationException(
                   "someProperty should not be more than 3");
           }

           return this.someProperty;
       }
   }
✓  private int someProperty = 1;

   public int SomeProperty
   {
       get
       {
           Debug.Assert(
               this.someProperty > 3,
               "someProperty should not be more than 3");

           return this.someProperty;
       }
   }
```

▸ Code Analysis CA1065

✴ A catch block **must not** be preceded by a blank line.

```
✗  try
   {
       // omitted
   }

   catch (FileNotFoundException)
```

```
    {
        // omitted
    }
✓   try
    {
        // omitted
    }
    catch (FileNotFoundException)
    {
        // omitted
    }
```

▶ StyleCop SA1510

✷ When an **ArgumentException** exception is thrown, it **must** pass the **message** and **param** arguments.

The message argument should indicate what went wrong and if possible, what must be done to fix the problem.

```
✗   public void SomeMethod(string value)
    {
        if (value == null)
        {
            throw new ArgumentNullException("value");
        }

        if (value.Length < 5)
        {
            throw new ArgumentException();
        }

        // omitted
    }
✓   public void SomeMethod(string value)
    {
        if (value == null)
        {
            throw new ArgumentNullException("value");
        }

        if (value.Length < 5)
        {
```

```
        throw new ArgumentException(
            "Argument should be at least 5 character long",
            "value");
    }

    // omitted
}
```

▸ Code Analysis CA2208

Fields

These related sections also apply to fields:

- Identifiers
- Scope

These are examples of valid declarations of a field:

```
✓ public static readonly double Phi = (1 + Math.Sqrt(5)) / 2;

✓ internal static readonly double Phi = (1 + Math.Sqrt(5)) / 2;

✓ internal readonly double Phi = (1 + Math.Sqrt(5)) / 2;

✓ protected internal static readonly double Phi =
      (1 + Math.Sqrt(5)) / 2;

✓ protected static readonly double Phi = (1 + Math.Sqrt(5)) / 2;

✓ private static readonly double Phi = (1 + Math.Sqrt(5)) / 2;

✓ private static double phi = (1 + Math.Sqrt(5)) / 2;

✓ private readonly double phi = (1 + Math.Sqrt(5)) / 2;

✓ private double phi = (1 + Math.Sqrt(5)) / 2;
```

✳ A non-private field **must** use Pascal case.

A field with any access modifier except private should use Pascal case.

```
✗ internal readonly double phi = (1 + Math.Sqrt(5)) / 2;

✓ internal readonly double Phi = (1 + Math.Sqrt(5)) / 2;
```

▸ StyleCop SA1300, SA1304, SA1307, SA1311

✳ A private field **must** use camel case.

A private field should use camel case, which indicates that the scope is not exposed outside the class.

```
✗  private readonly double Phi = (1 + Math.Sqrt(5)) / 2;

✓  private readonly double phi = (1 + Math.Sqrt(5)) / 2;
```

⊗ A private static readonly field should be in Pascal case.

▸ StyleCop SA1306

✳ A field **must** have the private scope unless it is readonly.

Fields should be private and exposed by properties. However, a readonly field can be exposed.

▸ Code Analysis CA1051, StyleCop SA1401

✳ A field name **must not** have a prefix that indicates scope.

Do not use s_, or m_ prefixes to indicate global, static, or private fields.

```
✗  private int m_indexItem;
   private static long s_radix;

✓  private int indexItem;
   private long radix;
```

▸ Code Analysis CA1504, StyleCop SA1308

✳ A field name **must not** begin with an underscore.

In C#, a private field should be differentiated from the public property by case.

```
✗  private int _someField;

✓  private int someField;
```

▸ StyleCop SA1309

* A private field that is encapsulated by a public property **should** have the same name but differ by case.

```
✔ [ContractPublicPropertyName("SomeProperty")]
  private int someProperty;

  public int SomeProperty
  {
      get
      {
          return this.someProperty;
      }
  }
```

* [Code Contracts] A private field that is encapsulated by public properties **must** always be decorated with the ContractPublicPropertyName attribute.

This attribute allows Code Contracts to access the private field. Without it, Code Contracts can only access the public property.

```
✘ private int someProperty;

  public int SomeProperty
  {
      get
      {
          return this.someProperty;
      }
  }
✔ [ContractPublicPropertyName("SomeProperty")]
  private int someProperty;

  public int SomeProperty
  {
      get
      {
          return this.someProperty;
      }
  }

  public void SomeMethod(int someValue)
  {
```

```
        Contract.Requires<ArgumentOutOfRange>(
            someValue > this.someProperty);

        // omitted
    }
```

✳ A private field that is not used **must** be removed.

There should be no unused private fields. If it is anticipated that the field will be used again later, it can be commented out.

```
✗  private int notUsed;

✓  ////private int notUsed;
```

▶ Code Analysis CA1823

✳ A class or struct that has an instance field that implements the IDisposable interface **should** also implement the IDisposable interface.

If an instance field implements the IDisposable interface, the class or struct that contains it should as well. In the Dispose method for the class or struct, it should call the Dispose method for the instance field. This makes it so that calling the Dispose method of the instance of the class or struct cleans up all of the resources that the instance allocates. If this is not implemented, the resources of the instance field continue to be consumed until garbage collected, even though the instance of the class is no longer being used. In the case of a FileStream, for example, this will hold the file open until garbage collected.

```
✗  public class SomeClass
    {
        // FileStream implements IDisposable
        private FileStream fileStream;

        public SomeClass()
        {
            this.fileStream = new FileStream(
                @"c:\temp\temp.txt",
                FileMode.Open);
        }
    }
```

```
✓ public class SomeClass : IDisposable
  {
      // FileStream implements IDisposable
      private FileStream fileStream;

      public SomeClass()
      {
          this.fileStream = new FileStream(
              @"c:\temp\temp.txt",
              FileMode.Open);
      }

      ~SomeClass()
      {
          this.Dispose(false);
      }

      public void Dispose()
      {
          this.Dispose(true);
          GC.SuppressFinalize(this);
      }

      protected virtual void Dispose(bool disposing)
      {
          if (disposing)
          {
              this.fileStream.Dispose();
          }
      }
  }
```

▶ Code Analysis CA1001

✳ A mutable reference-type field in an accessible class or struct **should not** be marked readonly.

A readonly modifier makes the contents of the field not mutable. With a reference type field, the field is not mutable, but the contents of the object the field references are mutable. Many programmers will interpret this incorrectly. The readonly modifier does not make it clear that the object is mutable.

This rule includes fields that are declared as arrays.

```
✗   public class PublicClass
    {
        internal readonly StringBuilder stringBuilder =
            new StringBuilder();
    }
✓   public class PublicClass
    {
        internal StringBuilder stringBuilder = new StringBuilder();
    }
```

▶ Code Analysis CA2104, CA2105

Files

Files inside a project must meet these rules.

✳ A file name **must** use Pascal case.

A file that is contained within a project must have a name in Pascal case.

```
✗   someclass.cs
✓   SomeClass.cs
```

✳ A file **must** have a header.

The header should have a layout similar to this:

```
✓   //------------------------------------------------------------
    // <copyright file="FileName.cs" company="Acme Corporation">
    //     Copyright © 2020 Acme Corporation
    // </copyright>
    // <summary>
    // This is a full and complete description of what this file does.
    // </summary>
    //------------------------------------------------------------
```

The lines with the hyphens at the top and bottom of the header should be exactly 140 characters long (to make this fit in the book, the font size was reduced for these two lines). This corresponds to the maximum line length. If a different line length maximum is used, the length of the line should be changed too. By sizing the window to the width of these lines, the maximum line length can be observed.

The file attribute in the header must match the file name. The company attribute must match the company name. The company name must be the same across the entire project. See the section on Copyright Notices for more details.

► StyleCop SA1633, SA1637, SA1638, SA1640, SA1641, SA1649

✳ A file header **must** have a copyright notice.

The file header must have a copyright notice. This notice should be standard across the entire project. See the section on Copyright Notices for more details on the form of the copyright notice.

► StyleCop SA1634, SA1635, SA1636

✳ A file header **should** have a summary that describes the purpose of the file.

► StyleCop SA1639

✳ A file **should** only contain a single class or struct.

Each class should be stored in their own file.

⊗ A number of very small, related classes may be contained within one file, such as the definition of a set of related exceptions. However, it is generally better to create a folder within the project and place each exception in a separate file in the folder.

► StyleCop SA1402

✳ A file **should** only contain one namespace.

All items in a file should be related, and therefore should be in only one namespace.

► StyleCop SA1403

✳ A line of a file **must** end with a CR/LF combination.

Although C# allows several kinds of line terminators, the only one that should be used is the CR/LF combination (U+000D followed by U+000A).

Formatting Code

* Elements of a type **must** appear in a file in a particular order.

   There are several criteria of sorting: the element kind, the scope, whether it is static, whether it is read-only, and the name of the element.

   Elements must appear in this order:

   1. Constants and Fields
   2. Constructors
   3. Destructors
   4. Delegates
   5. Events
   6. Enums
   7. Interfaces
   8. Properties
   9. Indexers
   10. Methods and Operators
   11. Structs
   12. Classes

   Then within each group, the items must be sorted by scope in this order:

   1. public
   2. internal
   3. protected-internal
   4. protected
   5. private

   Then within each group, items must be sorted in this order:

   1. Static elements
   2. Instance elements

   Then for constants and fields, items must be sorted in this order:

   1. Read-only elements (this includes all constants)

2. Non-read-only elements.

Then the items must be sorted by name using a case-insensitive comparison. While the other sorting is enforced by StyleCop rules, the sorting by name is not.

The drawback to using this ordering is that a change of any of the elements of sorting, such as changing a method's access from private to public, requires moving the code in the file. This makes viewing the history of that code in the version control system more difficult. The advantage is that a programmer will know approximately where a given block of code will appear within a file. The advantages outweigh the disadvantages.

▶ StyleCop SA1201, SA1202, SA1203, SA1204, SA1207, SA1214, SA1215

✳ **The keywords in the declaration of an element must appear in a particular order.**

The keywords must appear in this order:

- Access modifiers
- Static
- All other keywords

Having the access modifier first highlights the scope of the element, helping prevent giving an element more access than is necessary.

```
✗ static public void SomeMethod()
  {
      // omitted
  }
✓ public static void SomeMethod()
  {
      // omitted
  }
```

▶ StyleCop SA1206

✳ **A partial class must have an access modifier.**

```
✗ partial class SomeClass
  {
```

```
        // omitted
    }
✔ public partial class SomeClass
    {
        // omitted
    }
```

- ▶ StyleCop SA1205

✻ Each line of code **must** be no more than 140 characters long.

This length was chosen to allow printing of code using a Consolas 10 point typeface, using the landscape printing orientation on Letter (8½"x11") or A4 paper. While this is the recommended length, the programming team can standardize on any other length.

If the page header lines are 140 characters long, the code window easily can be sized to this width. Alternately, the Productivity Power Tools extension (a free download published by Microsoft) allows creating Column Guides that places a line at the proper location on the screen in the code window.

If a line is commented out with /////, then the line length is permitted to exceed the normal length by four characters, to allow for the comment characters. The comment characters presumably will be removed at some point, at which point the length will be correct.

✻ There **must not** be more than one consecutive blank line.

```
✗ private int someField1 = 0;


    private int someField2 = 1;
✔ private int someField1 = 0;

    private int someField2 = 1;
```

- ▶ StyleCop SA1507

✻ An opening brace **must not** be followed by a blank line.

```
✗ public class SomeClass
    {

```

```
        public void SomeMethod()
        {
            // omitted
        }
    }
✔ public class SomeClass
    {
        public void SomeMethod()
        {
            // omitted
        }
    }
```

- ▸ StyleCop SA1505

✴ A closing brace **must not** be preceded by a blank line.

```
✗ public class SomeClass
    {
        public void SomeMethod()
        {
            // omitted
        }

    }
✔ public class SomeClass
    {
        public void SomeMethod()
        {
            // omitted
        }
    }
```

- ▸ StyleCop SA1508

✴ An opening brace **must not** be preceded by a blank line.

```
✗ public class SomeClass
    {
        public void SomeMethod()

        {
            // omitted
```

```
        }
    }
✓ public class SomeClass
    {
        public void SomeMethod()
        {
            // omitted
        }
    }
```

▸ StyleCop SA1509

✴ A closing brace **must** be followed by a blank line.

A closing brace must be followed by a blank line. This opens the code
and makes it easier to read.

```
✗ if (value == 1)
    {
        // omitted
    }
    Console.WriteLine(value);
✓ if (value == 1)
    {
        // omitted
    }

    Console.WriteLine(value);
```

⊗ The while statement at the end of a do-while block is not preceded by
   a blank line.

▸ StyleCop SA1513

✴ The while statement at the end of a do-while block **must not**
be preceded by a blank line.

```
✗ do
    {
        // omitted
    }

    while (a == 2);
```

```
✔ do
  {
      // omitted
  }
  while (a == 2);
```

▸ StyleCop SA1511

✹ There **must not** be more than one consecutive white space characters.

⊗ Consecutive white space characters may appear at the beginning of a line. Consecutive whitespace characters may also appear in literal strings.

```
✗ public    void SomeMethod()
  {
      // omitted
  }
✔ public void SomeMethod()
  {
      // omitted
  }
```

▸ StyleCop SA1025

✹ There **must not** be extraneous white space at the end of the line.

```
✗ // _ is used to indicate spaces
  int value = 1;____
✔ int value = 1;
```

✹ There **must not** be blank lines at the beginning of a file.

There should not be any blank lines at the beginning of the file. The first line should be part of the file header.

▸ StyleCop SA1517

✹ There **must not** be blank lines at the end of a file.

There must not be any blank lines at the end of the file. The last line of code should end with the end of file character, indicated in the example below by the symbol ⬚. It is possible to see the end of file character in Visual Studio by selecting Edit ⇨ Advanced ⇨ View White Space.

```
✗ namespace SomeNameSpace
  {
      // omitted
  }


  ⬚

✓ namespace SomeNameSpace
  {
      // omitted
  }⬚
```

▸ StyleCop SA1518

✳ Adjacent elements **must** be separated by a blank line.

Two elements must be separated by a blank line. Most elements will be preceded by an XML comment, which requires a blank line before it. However, this rule includes the get and set of properties, which do not have any documentation requirements.

```
✓ private int someProperty = 0;

  public int SomeProperty
  {
      get
      {
          return this.someProperty;
      }
      set
      {
          this.someProperty = value;
      }
  }
✓ private int someProperty = 0;

  public int SomeProperty
  {
      get
      {
          return this.someProperty;
```

```
        }

    set
    {
        this.someProperty = value;
    }
}
```

▶ StyleCop SA1516

✳ The contents of do, for, foreach, if, and while statements **must** be surrounded by braces.

The C# syntax allows the do, for, foreach, if, and while statements to omit braces if only a single statement follow them. However, braces should always be included, even around a single statement. This improves readability of the code, and helps maintenance when a second statement is added.

The else clause of an if statement must also be enclosed by braces. However, an else if construct does not need additional braces between the else and if.

```
✗ if (a == 2)
      Console.WriteLine("two");
  else
      Console.WriteLine("Something else");

✓ if (a == 2)
  {
      Console.WriteLine("two");
  }
  else
  {
      Console.WriteLine("Something else");
  }

✓ if (a == 2)
  {
      Console.WriteLine("two");
  }
  else if (a == 3)
  {
      Console.WriteLine("three");
  }
  else
```

```
    {
        Console.WriteLine("Something else");
    }
```

▸ StyleCop SA1503

✳ An else block **must not** be preceded by a blank line.

```
✗ if (a == 2)
    {
        // omitted
    }

    else
    {
        // omitted
    }
✔ if (a == 2)
    {
        // omitted
    }
    else
    {
        // omitted
    }
```

▸ StyleCop SA1510

✳ Statements with braces **must** be written across multiple lines.

```
✗ if (value != null) { Console.WriteLine(value); }

✗ public void SomeMethod() { return; }

✔ if (value != null)
    {
        Console.WriteLine(value);
    }
✔ public void SomeMethod()
    {
        return;
    }
```

▶ StyleCop SA1501, SA1502

✳ Most keywords **must** be followed by a single space.

The following C# keywords must always be followed by a single space:

catch	fixed	for	foreach
from	group	if	in
into	join	let	lock
orderby	return	select	stackalloc
switch	throw	using	where
while	yield.		

```
✗  for(int value = 1; value < 100; value++)
   {
       // omitted
   }
✓  for (int value = 1; value < 100; value++)
   {
       // omitted
   }
```

▶ StyleCop SA1000.

✳ Some keywords **must not** be followed by a space.

The following keywords must not be followed by a space:

checked	default	sizeof	typeof	unchecked

These keywords have the appearance of being methods, so do not have a space after them.

```
✗  int size = sizeof (int);
✓  int size = sizeof(int);
```

▶ StyleCop SA1000.

✳ The new keyword **must** be followed by a single space.

```
✗ SomeClass someClass = new    SomeClass();

✓ SomeClass someClass = new SomeClass();
```

⊗ If creating a new array, there should be no space between the new keyword and the opening array bracket. This is infrequently used, as the new[] can be omitted in many cases.

```
✗ var array = new [] { 1, 2, 3 };

✓ var array = new[] { 1, 2, 3 };

✓ int[] array = { 1, 2, 3 };
```

▸ StyleCop SA1000, SA1026

✳ A comma **must not** be preceded by a space and **must** be followed by a space.

⊗ If a comma is the last character on a line, it must not followed by a space.

```
✗ private void TestFunction(int value,string description)
  {
      // omitted
  }

✓ private void TestFunction(int value, string description)
  {
      // omitted
  }
```

▸ StyleCop SA1001

✳ A semicolon **must not** be preceded by a space and **must** be followed by a space.

⊗ If a semicolon is the first character on a line, it may be preceded by white space. If it is the last character on a line, it must not be followed by a space.

```
✗ using System ;
```

```
✗  for (int i = 0 ; i < 10 ; i++)
   {
       // omitted
   }
✓  using System;
✓  for (int i = 0; i < 10; i++)
   {
       // omitted
   }
```

▶ StyleCop SA1002

✴ Most symbols **must** be surrounded by a space.

The following symbols must be surrounded by a space on either side:

- colons
- arithmetic operators
- assignment operators
- conditional operators
- logical operators
- relational operators
- shift operators
- lambda operators

⊗ If the operator appears at the beginning of a line, it may be preceded by white space. If the operator is appears at the end of line, it should not be followed by any white space.

```
✗  int x = 4 +3;
✗  int x = 4 + 3;
```

▶ StyleCop SA1003

✴ Unary operators **must** be preceded by a space and have no trailing white space.

A unary operator must not be the last character on a line.

⊗ If the operator immediately follows an opening parenthesis or bracket, then it is not preceded by a space.

```
✗  int x = - 4;

✓  int x = -4;

✗  int x = Math.Pow( -4, 2);

✓  int x = Math.Pow(-4, 2);
```

▸ StyleCop SA1003, SA1021, SA1022

✳ An opening parenthesis **must not** have white space before or after it.

There are a number of exceptions to this rule.

⊗ If the keyword before the parenthesis is for, foreach, if, or while, it must be preceded by a single space.

⊗ If the parenthesis is preceded by an operator in an expression, it must be preceded by a single space.

⊗ If the parenthesis is the first character on the line, it may be preceded by white space.

```
✗  this.SomeMethod ( someValue);

✓  this.SomeMethod(someValue);

✗  if(someValue == 1)
   {
       // omitted
   }

✓  if (someValue == 1)
   {
       // omitted
   }

✗  int someValue = ( a + b)* ( c + d);

✓  int someValue = (a + b) * (c + d);
```

▸ StyleCop SA1008

✳ A closing parenthesis **must not** have white space before it and **must** be followed by a single space.

There are some exceptions to the space after the parenthesis:

⊗ If it comes at the end of a cast, there should be no space after the closing parenthesis.

⊗ If the next character after a parenthesis is opening or closing parenthesis or square bracket, or a semicolon or comma, there should be no space after the closing parenthesis.

```
✗ int someValue =(a + b ) *(c + d ) ;

✓ int someValue = (a + b) * (c + d);

✗ int someValue = (int) a;

✓ int someValue = (int)a;
```

▶ StyleCop SA1009

✱ An opening square bracket **must not** have white space before or after it.

⊗ A square bracket at the beginning of a line may have white space before it.

```
✗ int [] someField = { 0 };

✓ int[] someField = { 0 };
```

▶ StyleCop SA1010, SA1016

✱ A closing square bracket **must not** have white space before it and **must** be followed by a space.

⊗ A closing square bracket may be preceded by white space if it is the first character on the line.

⊗ A closing square bracket must not have white space after it if it is the last character of a line, it is followed by a closing bracket or an opening parenthesis, it is followed by a comma or semicolon, or it is followed by certain types of operator symbols.

```
✗ int[]someField = { 0 };

✓ int[] someField = { 0 };
```

▶ StyleCop SA1011, SA1017

116

✳ An opening curly brace **must** be preceded and followed by a space.

> ⊗ An opening curly brace must not have a space before it if it is preceded by an opening parenthesis.

> ⊗ An opening curly brace must not be followed by a space if it is the last character on the line.

```
✗ int[] array = {1, 2, 3 };

✓ int[] array = { 1, 2, 3 };
```

▸ StyleCop SA1012

✳ A closing curly brace **must** be preceded and followed by a space.

> ⊗ A closing curly brace must not have a preceding space if it is the first character on a line.

> ⊗ A closing curly brace must not have a following space if it is the last character of a line.

```
✗ int[] array = { 1, 2, 3};

✓ int[] array = { 1, 2, 3 };
```

▸ StyleCop SA1013

✳ An opening generic angle bracket **must not** be preceded or followed by white space.

> ⊗ An opening generic angle bracket may be preceded by white space if it is the first character on a line.

```
✗ public class RuleSA1014Fail< T>
  {
      // omitted
  }

✓ public class RuleSA1014Fail<T>
  {
      // omitted
  }
```

▸ StyleCop SA1014

117

✳ A closing generic angle bracket **must not** be preceded or followed by white space.

⊗ A closing generic angle bracket may be preceded by white space if it is the first character of a line.

```
✗ public class RuleSA1015Fail<T >
  {
      // omitted
  }
✓ public class RuleSA1015Fail<T>
  {
      // omitted
  }
```

▶ StyleCop SA1015

✳ There **must not** be white space between an increment or decrement operator and the item being incremented or decremented.

```
✗ value ++;
✓ value++;
```

▶ StyleCop SA1020

✳ A dereference symbol **must** be spaced correctly.

The asterisk dereference symbol in a type declaration must not be preceded by a space and must be followed by a space.

The asterisk dereference symbol outside of a type declaration must be preceded by a space and must not be followed by a space.

```
✗ unsafe
  {
      int * value = null;
      int blah = * value;
  }
✓ unsafe
  {
      int* value = null;
```

```
      int blah = *value;
   }
```

▸ StyleCop SA1023

✳ More than one statement **must not** appear on a single line.

```
✗ int value1 = 1; int value2 = 2;

✓ int value1 = 1;

  int value2 = 2;
```

▸ StyleCop SA1107

✳ Code **should not** contain empty statements.

The code cannot contain two consecutive semicolons, whether
separated by whitespace or not. A block cannot begin with just an empty
statement.

```
✗ Console.WriteLine();;

✗ public void SomeMethod()
  {
      ;
  }

✓ Console.WriteLine();

✓ public void SomeMethod()
  {
  }
```

▸ StyleCop SA1106

✳ A reference to a member **must** be referenced by this, base, or
a variable, or the type name.

Each reference to a member of a class or struct must be prefixed with an
indication of where that member is found, followed by the period. If the
member is an instance member of the current class or struct, then
reference it by this. If the member is a static member of a class or struct,
then reference it by the type name. If it is an instance member of
another class or struct, then reference it by a variable name. If it is a

member of the base class of the current class and there is a member by the same name in the current class, then reference it by **base**.

This makes it easy to identify references to members, because all members are prefixed, whereas local variables will never be prefixed.

Members include fields, as well as method calls and properties.

```
✗ private int someValue = 1;

  public int SomeProperty
  {
      get;
      set;
  }

  public void SomeMethod()
  {
      someValue = 2;
      SomeOtherMethod();
      SomeProperty = 1;
  }

  private void SomeOtherMethod()
  {
      // omitted
  }
✓ private int someValue = 1;

  public void SomeMethod()
  {
      this.someValue = 2;
      this.SomeOtherMethod();
      this.SomeProperty = 1;
  }

  private void SomeOtherMethod()
  {
      // omitted
  }
✗ public static SomeClass
  {
      private static int someValue = 1;
```

```
        public static int SomeProperty
        {
            get;
            set;
        }

        public static void SomeMethod()
        {
            someValue = 2;
            SomeOtherMethod();
            SomeProperty = 1;
        }

        private static void SomeOtherMethod()
        {
            // omitted
        }
    }
✔ public static SomeClass
    {
        private static int someValue = 1;

        public static int SomeProperty
        {
            get;
            set;
        }

        public static void SomeMethod()
        {
            SomeClass.someValue = 2;
            SomeClass.SomeOtherMethod();
            SomeClass.SomeProperty = 1;
        }

        private static void SomeOtherMethod()
        {
            // omitted
        }
    }
```

▶ StyleCop SA1101, SA1126

✳ A reference to a member **must not** use base unless there is a local implementation of the member.

Calling a method with base should only occur when there is a local method that overrides the base method, and the base method needs to be called bypassing the local method. Otherwise, call the method with this.

```
✗  public class SomeClass
   {
       public virtual void SomeVirtualMethod()
       {
           // omitted
       }
   }

   public class SomeClassDerived : SomeClass
   {
       public void SomeMethod()
       {
           base.SomeVirtualMethod();
       }
   }
✓  public class SomeClass
   {
       public virtual void SomeVirtualMethod()
       {
           // omitted
       }
   }

   public class SomeClassDerived : SomeClass
   {
       public void SomeMethod()
       {
           this.SomeVirtualMethod();
       }
   }
✓  public class SomeClass
   {
       public virtual void SomeVirtualMethod()
       {
           // omitted
```

```
        }
    }

    public class SomeClassDerived : SomeClass
    {
        public override void SomeVirtualMethod()
        {
            // omitted
        }

        public void SomeMethod()
        {
            base.SomeVirtualMethod();
        }
    }
```

▶ StyleCop SA1100

✳ A member access symbol **must not** have white space.

The this, base, *object*, or *typename* member access must not have white space before or after the period.

⊗ In code that must span multiple lines, white space at the start of a line before the access symbol is permitted.

```
✗ this .value = 6;

✓ this.value = 6;
```

▶ StyleCop SA1019

✳ A representation of a zero length string **must** use string.Empty.

A zero length string must use string.Empty, and must not use "" or String.Empty. The capitalized String.Empty requires a using declaration for the System namespace.

```
✗ private string value = "";

✗ private string value = String.Empty;

✓ private string value = string.Empty;
```

▶ StyleCop SA1122

✳ The nullable type symbol (?) **must** be used.

This provides a standard way of expressing nullable types in code.

```
✗  private Nullable<int> value = null;

✔  private int? value = null;
```

▸ StyleCop SA1125

✳ The nullable type symbol (?) **must not** be preceded by a space.

```
✗  private int ? value = null;

✔  private int? value = null;
```

▸ StyleCop SA1018

✳ Indenting **must** be formed by tab characters.

This is one of the most hotly contested issues in coding. A programming team may choose to indent using spaces rather than tabs. However, all code must be consistent.

✳ A tab **must** be defined to be the equivalent of four spaces when determining line length.

✳ Braces for multi-line statements **must not** share lines with other code.

Opening and closing braces may only have white space preceding them, and nothing after them on the same line.

```
✗  for (int count = 1; count < 10; count++) {
       // omitted
   }

✔  for (int count = 1; count < 10; count++)
   {
       // omitted
   }
```

This is the default brace style used by Visual Studio and is very readable. It is sometimes called the Allman or BSD style. There are many styles of indenting code discussed in the article Indenting Style on Wikipedia (https://en.wikipedia.org/wiki/Indent_style). Which indenting style is used is far less important than having everyone on the team use the same style.

⊗ Braces may appear on the same line as other code when defining defaults for arrays and collections if the data set is small.

```
✔ private int[] setOfData = new { 1, 2, 3, 5, 7, 11 };
```

⊗ A closing brace may appear on the same line of code in the C# version 6 specification of the default value for an Auto property.

```
✔ public int SomeProperty
  {
      get;
      set;
  } = 1;
```

▶ StyleCop SA1500

✳ Braces used for multi-line statements **must** be indented to the level of the code that precedes it.

```
✗ public void SomeMethod()
      {
      // omitted
      }
✔ public void SomeMethod()
  {
      // omitted
  }
```

✳ Colons **must** have appropriate spacing around them.

A colon is always followed by a single space unless it is the last character in a line. A colon following a label is not preceded by white space. All other colons are preceded by a single space.

```
✗ public class SomeClass<T>:SomeOtherClass Where T:SomeType
  {
      // omitted
  }
```

```
✗  public void SomeMethod()
   {
       // omitted
       someLabel :
       /omitted
   }

✓  public class SomeClass<T> : SomeOtherClass Where T : SomeType
   {
       // omitted
   }

✓  public void SomeMethod()
   {
       // omitted
       someLabel:
       /omitted
   }
```

▶ StyleCop SA1024

✴ The opening brace and closing brace of a block **must** be indented to the same level.

```
✗  public void SomeMethod()
   {
       // omitted
       }

✓  public void SomeMethod()
   {
       // omitted
   }
```

✴ The contents of a block **must** be indented from the braces that define the block by one tab stop.

```
✗  public void SomeMethod()
   {
   Console.WriteLine();
   }

✓  public void SomeMethod()
   {
```

```
        Console.WriteLine();
    }
```

* A line of code that is continued onto multiple physical lines **must** be indented from the first physical line by one tab stop.

When a line is continued onto multiple physical lines, the continuation lines should be indented by one tab stop from the first line.

```
✗   if (string.Compare(
    "abc",
    "def",
    false,
    CultureInfo.CurrentCulture) == 0))
    {
        // omitted
    }
✓   if (string.Compare(
        "abc",
        "def",
        false,
        CultureInfo.CurrentCulture) == 0))
    {
        // omitted
    }
```

Generics

* A generic type parameter **should** start with the capital letter T.

In most cases, this will be just the letter T, but if there are multiple generic parameters, they should be followed by a description.

```
✗   public class SomeClass<Alpha>
    {
        // omitted
    }
✓   public class SomeClass<T>
    {
```

```
        // omitted
    }
```

▸ Code Analysis CA1715

✳ There **should not** be more than two generic types parameters declared on the same method or type.

```
✗ public class SomeClass<TType1,TType2,TType3>
    {
        // omitted
    }

✓ public class SomeClass<TType1, TType2>
    {
        // omitted
    }
```

▸ Code Analysis CA1005

Identifiers

Identifiers are used to name items. Identifiers include namespaces, types, members, and parameters.

✳ An identifier **must** be spelled correctly.

Each part of an identifier should be spelled correctly. In a Pascal or camel cased identifier, each part of the identifier should be spelled using a standard dictionary.

Add domain specific words to the CodeAnalysisDictionary included into the project.

```
✗ public void SoomeMethod()
    {
        // omitted
    }
✓ public void SomeMethod()
    {
        // omitted
    }
```

▸ Code Analysis CA1704

✳ Two elements of the same type at the same scope **must not** differ only by case.

Some .NET languages, such as Visual Basic, are case insensitive. Two elements that differ only by case are impossible to distinguish in these languages.

This applies to namespaces, parameters, classes, structs, properties, methods, and other similar items.

⊗ A property and a private field that stores the value of the property should differ only by case. However, a private field in C# will never be exposed to another language.

```
✗  public void Somemethod()
   {
       // omitted
   }

   public void SomeMethod()
   {
       // omitted
   }
```

▸ Code Analysis CA1708

✳ An identifier name **must not** include the type name.

Different languages use different words for the same type name. For example, the single data type in Visual Basic is the same as the float data type in C#, thus putting the type name into the variable name is confusing in other environments.

```
✗  double doubleStorage;

✓  double storage;
```

The prohibited use of type names in identifiers depends on the semantics of the use, however. For example, it is perfectly allowable to use double in an identifier to mean twice something rather than the data type name.

```
✓  int doubleInputAmount = 2 * inputAmount;
```

There are a few cases, such as Convert methods that change between data types, which will need to have the type name in them. Use these Universal Type Names in Convert method names:

✗C# Type Name	✓Universal Type Name
bool	Boolean
byte	Byte
char	Char
double	Double
float	Single
int	Int32
long	Int64
object	Object
sbyte	SByte
short	Int16
string	String
uint	UInt32
ulong	UInt64
ushort	UInt16

```
✗ // Converts the current data type to floating point
  public float ToFloat(IFormatProvider provider)
  {
      // omitted
  }
✓ // Converts the current data type to floating point
  public float ToSingle(IFormatProvider provider)
  {
      // omitted
  }
```

▸ Code Analysis CA1720

✳ An identifier name **must not** include an underscore.

```
✗ TimeSpan zero_date;
✓ TimeSpan zeroDate;
```

⊗ IDE generated events such as ButtonClose_Click may be kept in their original form.

▸ Code Analysis CA1707, StyleCop SA1310

✳ An identifier name must not use Hungarian type notation.

```
✗  string strValue;

✓  string value;
```

▸ StyleCop SA1305

✳ An identifier name should not include abbreviations and contractions.

Normally a word should be completely spelled out.

⊗ There are some cases where an abbreviation is actually more standard than the word or words it abbreviates. In that case, an abbreviation is permitted. In addition, well-known acronyms such as HTML and UI can be used.

In the examples below, AD is much more commonly used than Anno Domini is, and UI is a frequently used acronym for User Interface.

```
✗  double evtHorizon;
   int annoDominiYear;
   Form userInterface;
   bool cantRead;

✓  double eventHorizon;
   int adYear;
   Form ui;
   bool cannotRead;
```

✳ An identifier name should not match a keyword.

For identifiers, it is permissible to use names that are compounds of these names. Do not use any capitalization of these identifiers. The identifiers are listed in Appendix A: Prohibited Identifier Names

```
✗  public class AddHandler
   {
       // omitted
   }

✗  public class addhandler
   {
       // omitted
   }
```

```
✔  public class NewAddHandler
   {
       // omitted
   }
```

▶ Code Analysis CA1716

✳ An identifier **should not** be prefixed with the verbatim character (@).

The verbatim identifier is used to make what would normally be a keyword in C#, such as private, be treated as a normal variable.

```
✗  private int @private;
```

⊗ When creating a library that is to be used with a different .NET programming language than C#, there might be identifiers that require the verbatim character.

✳ An identifier of certain types **should** end in a specific suffix.

Identifiers of a certain types should end in specific suffix shown in the table in Appendix B: Suffixes for Certain Types.

```
✗  public class SomeClass : EventArgs
   {
       // omitted
   }
✔  public class SomeClassEventArgs : EventArgs
   {
       // omitted
   }
```

▶ Code Analysis CA1710

✳ Identifiers not of a specific type **should not** end in specific suffixes.

Unless an identifier is of a specific type, it should not end in the specified suffix shown in the table in Appendix B: Suffixes for Certain Types.

In addition, the following suffixes should never be used: Delegate, Enum, Ex, Impl.

```
✗   public class SomeCollection
    {
        // omitted
    }
✓   public class SomeClass
    {
        // omitted
    }
```

▶ Code Analysis CA1711

Indexers

These related sections also apply to indexers:

- Identifiers
- Methods
- Scope

✳ An indexer **should not** be multi-dimensional.

Instead of a multi-dimensional indexer, use a method.

```
✗   public int this[int large, int small]
    {
        get
        {
            // omitted
        }
    }
✓   public int GetValue(int large, int small)
    {
        // omitted
    }
```

▶ Code Analysis CA1023

✳ An indexer **should** use an integral or string type.

An index should use an integral type (short, int, long) or string. If it must be another type, change the indexer to be a method.

```
✘  public int this[double index]
   {
       get
       {
           // omitted
       }
   }
✔  public int this[int index]
   {
       get
       {
           // omitted
       }
   }
```

▶ Code Analysis CA1043

✱ The opening bracket of an indexer parameter list **must** appear on the same line as the declaration.

```
✘  public int this
       [int index]
   {
       get
       {
           // omitted
       }
   }
✔  public int this[
       int index]
   {
       get
       {
           // omitted
       }
   }
```

▶ StyleCop SA1110

✳ The closing bracket of an indexer parameter list **must** appear on the same line as the last parameter or the line of the opening bracket if there are no parameters.

```
✗ public int this
      [
          int index
      ]
  {
      get
      {
          // omitted
      }
  }
✓ public int this[
      int index]
  {
      get
      {
          // omitted
      }
  }
```

▶ StyleCop SA1111, SA1112

Interfaces

These related sections also apply to interfaces:

- Identifiers
- Scope
- Types

✳ An interface name **must** use Pascal case.

```
✓ internal interface IRuntimeFieldInfo
  {
      // omitted
  }
```

▶ Code Analysis CA1709, StyleCop SA1300

✴ An interface name **must** start with the capital letter I.

Interfaces must begin with a capital I.

```
✗  internal interface RuntimeFieldInfo
   {
       // omitted
   }

✓  internal interface IRuntimeFieldInfo
   {
       // omitted
   }
```

⊗ There are some interfaces that must be used with external libraries
such as COM or the Windows API that do not begin with letter I. In
those cases, the interface must be enclosed in a class with a name
that ends in the suffix NativeMethods.

```
✓  internal class WindowsNativeMethods
   {
       internal interface RuntimeFieldInfo
       {
           // omitted
       }
   }
```

It is very useful that an interface begin with the letter I, since a class can
inherit from only a single other class, but can implement several
interfaces. On the line where the class is declared, this rule helps identify
which identifiers identify classes and which are interfaces.

▸ Code Analysis CA1715, StyleCop SA1302

✴ A class that is merely a concrete implementation of an
interface **should** have the same name as the interface
without the initial letter I.

```
✓  public interface ICity
   {
       // omitted
   }

   public class City : ICity
   {
```

```
    // omitted
}
```

⊗ There are plenty of exceptions to this rule. However, this is the default name to use unless some other name would make the code more clear.

✳ An interface declaration **must not** be empty.

An empty interface declaration does not define a contract. Sometimes an empty interface is used to identify classes for use with reflection. In those cases, an attribute should be used instead.

```
✗ public interface ICity
  {
  }

✓ public interface ICity
  {
      void ShutOffPower();
  }
```

▶ Code Analysis CA1040

LINQ

✳ A LINQ query **must not** contain blank lines.

```
✗ var even =
      from i in numbers
      where i % 2 == 0

      select i;

✓ var even =
      from i in numbers
      where i % 2 == 0
      select i;
```

▶ StyleCop SA1102

✳ A LINQ query **must** have a line break after the assignment.

The additional lines are all indented one tab stop. This makes all the lines of the LINQ query have the same left margin.

```
✗  var even = from i in numbers
       where i % 2 == 0
       select i;

✓  var even =
       from i in numbers
       where i % 2 == 0
       select i;
```

✱ A LINQ query **must** have each clause on a separate line.

```
✗  var even =
       from i in numbers
       where i % 2 == 0 select i;

✓  var even =
       from i in numbers
       where i % 2 == 0
       select i;
```

▶ StyleCop SA1103, SA1104, SA1105

Methods

These related sections also apply to methods:

- Identifiers
- Parameters
- Return Values
- Scope

✱ Method names **must** use Pascal case.

```
✗  private void someMethod()
   {
       // omitted
   }

✓  private void SomeMethod()
   {
       // omitted
   }
```

▶ Code Analysis CA1709, StyleCop SA1300

✱ Multiple methods names **must not** differ only by case.

While C# allows two methods to differ only by case, this is confusing. Furthermore, when used in public methods, it causes difficulty calling the code from case insensitive languages such as Visual Basic.

```
✗  private void SomeMethod()
   {
       // omitted
   }

   private void Somemethod()
   {
       // omitted
   }
```

✱ Methods that do not reference the instance of a class **should** be marked static.

Methods that do not reference the instance of the class, usually via this, should be marked static. There is a distinct performance gain from not using instance members.

After marking a method as static, the compiler will emit nonvirtual calls to the method, which will prevent a check at runtime to make sure that the current object pointer is non-null. This can result in a measurable performance gain.

```
✗  public class SomeClass
   {
       private int someField;

       public void SomeMethod()
       {
           // Code that does not reference "this"
       }
   }
✓  public class SomeClass
   {
       private int someField;

       public static void SomeMethod()
       {
           // Code that does not reference "this"
```

```
            }
        }

✓   public class SomeClass
    {
        private int someField;

        public void SomeMethod()
        {
            int someVariable = this.someField;

            // omitted
        }
    }
```

▶ Code Analysis CA1822

✳ Static methods **should not** be used in generic classes.

In a generic class, do not declare static methods. The calling technique requires passing the type on the class, rather than the method. Remove the generic type argument from the class, and add it to the method. Alternately, change the method to be an instance method.

```
✗   public static class SomeClass<T>
    {
        public static void StaticMethod(T type)
        {
            // omitted
        }
    }

✓   public static class SomeClass
    {
        public static void SomeMethod<T>(T type)
        {
            // omitted
        }
    }

✓   public class SomeClass<T>
    {
        public void SomeMethod(T type)
        {
            // omitted
```

```
        }
    }
```

▶ Code Analysis CA1000

Namespaces

These related sections also apply to namespaces:

- Identifiers

✷ A namespace name **must** use Pascal case.

```
✓ namespace Acme.RpnCalculator
  {
      // omitted
  }
```

▶ Code Analysis CA1709, StyleCop SA1300

✷ Two namespace names **must not** differ only by case.

```
✗ namespace Acme.RpnCalculator
  {
  }

  namespace Acme.Rpncalculator
  {
  }
```

✷ A namespace name **should** use the pattern
CompanyName.TechnologyName[.Feature][.Design].

If the company name is long, use a consistent acceptable shortened
version or acronym. Business form identifiers, such as Corporation, LLC,
Trust, Limited, etc. are usually omitted. See the section on Company
Name for more details.

```
✗ namespace AcmeCorporationInternational.BusinessLibrary
  {
      // omitted
  }
✗ namespace AcmeCorporation.BusinessLibrary
  {
```

```
        // omitted
    }
✓ namespace ACI.BusinessLibrary
    {
        // omitted
    }
✓ namespace Acme.BusinessLibrary
    {
        // omitted
    }
```

Follow the capitalization of the company name, even if it is not Pascal case.

```
✗ namespace Aci.BusinessLibrary
    {
        // omitted
    }
✓ namespace ACI.BusinessLibrary
    {
        // omitted
    }
```

Namespace should match the organization of the code, not the organization of the company writing the code. Organizing code by company hierarchy tends to break down after the next company reorganization.

```
✗ namespace Acme.DevelopmentUnit
    {
        // omitted
    }

    namespace Acme.BusinessUnit
    {
        // omitted
    }
```

✳ A namespace name **should** use a plural form.

A namespace normally contains more than one type inside it, therefore should have a name that indicates that it contains multiple types.

```
✗  namespace Acme.Form
   {
       // omitted
   }
✓  namespace Acme.Forms
   {
       // omitted
   }
```

✳ A namespace with only a few types inside them **should** be consolidated with another namespace.

A namespace with only a few types in it usually means the granularity of the namespaces is too small. The namespace should be consolidated with another namespace.

⊗ There are times where a namespace will be expanded later, where it would be appropriate to have a small namespace now. There may be other reasons for small namespaces. Violations of this rule should be carefully reviewed.

⊗ There may be a very small project that only has a few types in it. In such a case, the Code Analysis warning may be suppressed.

▸ Code Analysis CA1020

Native Methods

There are times where the code will need to interact with other environments than the .NET framework, such as the Windows API. Those other environments may have names that do not match the conventions given here. In such cases, place the methods, interfaces, and other items that need to interact with those external environments into a NativeMethods class.

✳ A NativeMethods class **must** have a name suffixed with NativeMethods.

```
✓  internal class WindowsNativeMethods
   {
       // definitions that violate the normal naming rules
   }
```

StyleCop ignores naming violations that occur within a NativeMethods class. The class can be named just **NativeMethods**.

The access modifier on a NativeMethods class should be internal. If there is a library of native methods that needs to be accessed by other libraries, then use the **InternalsVisibleTo** assembly attribute in the AssemblyInfo.cs file to make the native methods available to the other libraries.

```
✔  [assembly: InternalsVisibleTo("Acme.Financials, PublicKey="0024...")]
```

Object Names

✳ An object that represents a dialog **must** have a name prefixed with **Dialog**.

Operator Overloading

✳ An operator **must not** be overloaded to perform a task that is not equivalent to the operator it is overloading.

For example, the plus sign (+) operator must perform an addition or concatenation operation. The plus sign operator must not be overloaded to perform multiplication. Overloading the << operator to perform a console write operation is wrong, as well. Do not make operators perform tasks that should be implemented with methods.

✳ A public or protected member that implements addition or subtraction overloads **should** also implement the equals overload.

▶ Code Analysis CA1013

✳ Reference types **should not** overload the == operator.

On reference types, the **Equals** operator compares the references to see if they point to the same object. The default behavior of the **Equals** operator is usually correct.

```
✗  public class SomeClass
   {
       public int Val
       {
```

```
            get;
            set;
        }

        public static bool operator ==( SomeClass c1, SomeClass c2)
        {
            return c1.Val == c2.Val;
        }
    }
```

▶ Code Analysis CA1046

✳ When overloading an operator, there **must** be a space between **operator** and the overload symbol.

```
✗ public static string operator~(SomeClass value)
    {
        // omitted
    }
✓ public static string operator ~(SomeClass value)
    {
        // omitted
    }
```

▶ StyleCop SA1007

Parameters

These related sections also apply to parameters:

- Identifiers

✳ Parameter names **must** use camel case.

```
✗ public void SomeMethod(int ItemCount)
    {
        // omitted
    }
✓ public void SomeMethod(int itemCount)
    {
        // omitted
    }
```

* Multiple parameters names in the same method declaration **must not** differ only by case.

   While multiple parameters having the same name with different casing is allowed by C#, it causes problems if used in code that accessed by a case insensitive language such as Visual Basic. It is also makes it confusing to read the code.

```
✗ private void SomeMethod(int itemCount, int itemcount)
  {
      // omitted
  }
```

* A special prefix or suffix **must not** be used to mark value parameters, reference parameters, output parameters, or parameter arrays.

```
✗ public void SomeMethod(ref int refItemCount)
  {
      // omitted
  }

✓ public void SomeMethod(ref int itemCount)
  {
      // omitted
  }
```

* In public or protected methods, optional arguments **should not** be used.

   Instead, create overloaded methods, and pass the default value to the version of the method that has the most arguments.

```
✗ public void SomeMethod(int arg = 1)
  {
      // omitted
  }

✓ public void SomeMethod()
  {
      SomeMethod(1);
  }

  public void SomeMethod(int arg)
```

```
{
    // omitted
}
```

Optional arguments are inserted by the compiler at the place where the call occurs in the compiled code. The Common Language Specification (CLS) does not require that all compilers support optional arguments. Furthermore, changing defaults is not considered a binary breaking change. When the defaults are changed to new values, the calling code in another assembly will still use the old values, without notification, until it is recompiled with a reference to the new library. This can lead to very difficult to discover bugs, as the source code does not indicate what is happening. In any piece of code exposed outside the project, optional arguments should be avoided.

▶ Code Analysis CA1026

✳ Out parameters **should not** be used.

If only one item is returned from a method, make it the return value.

Out parameters are used when two or more values must be returned from a method. Wherever possible, however, out parameters should be avoided. Instead, consider returning a struct that has all of the returned items in it.

```
✗  private void Divide(int dividend, int divisor, out double output)
   {
       output = dividend / divisor;
   }

✓  private double Divide(int dividend, int divisor)
   {
       return dividend / divisor;
   }

✗  private void Divide(
       int dividend,
       int divisor,
       out int quotient,
       out int remainder)
   {
       quotient = (int)(dividend / divisor);
       remainder = dividend % divisor;
   }
```

```
✓  internal struct Result
   {
       public Result(int quotient, int remainder)
       {
           this.Quotient = quotient;
           this.Remainder = remainder;
       }

       internal int Quotient
       {
           get;
           private set;
       }

       public int Remainder
       {
           get;
           private set;
       }
   }

   private Result Divide(int dividend, int divisor)
   {
       return new Result(
           (int)(dividend / divisor),
           dividend % divisor);
   }
```

▸ Code Analysis CA1021

✳ Ref parameters **should not** be used.

Ref parameters change the value passed in. Wherever possible, return the changed value, rather using the Ref parameter. If two or more values need to be returned, create a struct or object and pass back the values as properties.

```
✗  public void SomeMethod(ref string item)
   {
       item += "ABCDE";
   }

✓  public string SomeMethod(string item)
   {
```

```
            return item + "ABCDE";
    }

✗   public void SomeMethod(ref string item1, ref string item2)
    {
        item1 += "ABCDE";
        item2 += "FGHIJ";
    }

✓   internal struct SomeStruct
    {
        public SomeStruct(string item1, string item2)
        {
            this.Item1 = item1;
            this.Item2 = item2;
        }

        public string Item1
        {
            get;
            private set;
        }

        public string Item2
        {
            get;
            private set;
        }
    }

    // omitted

    public SomeStruct SomeMethod(string item1, string item2)
    {
        return new SomeStruct(item1 + "ABCDE", item2 + "FGHIJ");
    }
```

▶ Code Analysis CA1045

✳ A ref parameter **should not** be the type System.Object or object in an externally visible method.

A ref parameter is not recommended. However, if one is used, its type should not be System.Object or object. Use a generic method instead so that the actual data type can be inferred, which is more efficient.

```
✗ internal void SomeMethod(ref object item)
  {
      // omitted
  }

✔ internal void SomeMethod<T>(ref T item)
  {
      // omitted
  }
```

▶ Code Analysis CA1007

✳ A parameter that represents a URI **should** use the System.Uri type, not a string.

A parameter that represents a Uniform Resource Identifier (URI) should be declared with the System.Uri class, not a string. (See RFC 3305, https://tools.ietf.org/html/rfc3305 and related RFCs). A Uniform Resource Locator (URL) is a kind of URI. A string representation of a URI is liable to have parsing or encoding errors that lead to security vulnerabilities.

⊗ A method that accepts a string URI may be allowed, as long as it parses the string into a URI, then calls an overload of the method that accepts a URI.

```
✗ public void SomeMethod(string uri)
  {
      // omitted
  }

✔ public void SomeMethod(Uri uri)
  {
      // omitted
  }

✔ public void SomeMethod(Uri uri)
  {
      // omitted
  }

  public void SomeMethod(string uri)
  {
      Uri uriParsed = new Uri(uri);
```

```
        SomeMethod(uriParsed);
    }
```

▶ Code Analysis CA1054, CA1057

✳ **A reference type parameter in a public method should** be checked for null.

Before using a reference type, it should be checked for null before being used. If the value is null, then some appropriate action should be taken, which might be to do nothing. If a parameter value is null, it is also valid to throw an **ArgumentNullException**.

```
✗  public void SomeMethod(string item)
   {
       int length = item.Length;

       // omitted
   }

✓  public void SomeMethod(string item)
   {
       int length = 0;
       if (item != null)
       {
           length = item.Length;

           // omitted
       }
   }

✓  public void SomeMethod(string item)
   {
       if (item == null)
       {
           throw new ArgumentNullException("item");
       }

       int length = item.Length;

       // omitted
   }
```

The C# version 6 null conditional operator (?.), sometimes combined with the null-coalescing operator (??), can make coding around possible nulls easier.

```
✔ public void SomeMethod(string item)
  {
      int length = item?.Length ?? 0;

      // omitted
  }
```

▶ Code Analysis CA1062

✳ Base types **should** be passed as parameters.

If the method does not use any of the specific properties or methods of a
derived type, then use the base type for the parameter. This makes the
method useful under a wider set of circumstances.

```
✘ public bool SomeMethod(FileStream fileStream)
  {
      bool result = false;
      if (fileStream != null)
      {
          result = fileStream.CanRead;
      }

      return result;
  }
✔ public bool SomeMethod(Stream stream)
  {
      bool result = false;
      if (stream != null)
      {
          result = stream.CanRead;
      }

      return result;
  }
```

▶ Code Analysis CA1011

✳ Repetitive parameters **should** be replaced by a params array.

Parameters that are similar to each other should be replaced by a
params array. If needed, check to see if a certain number of items are
passed.

```
✗  public void SomeMethod(
        object box1,
        object box2,
        object box3,
        object box4,
        object box5)
   {
       // omitted
   }
✓  public void SomeMethod(params object[] box)
   {
       // possible checks for box != null
       // and box.Length == 5

       //omitted
   }
```

▶ Code Analysis CA1025

✱ A parameter name **should not** match the name of the method.

A parameter name should not match the name of the method regardless of the casing.

```
✗  public void SomeMethod(int someMethod)
   {
       // omitted
   }
✓  public void SomeMethod(int someValue)
   {
       // omitted
   }
```

▶ Code Analysis CA1005

✱ A parameter name in an overridden method **should** match the name in the base method.

When overriding a method, a parameter name should match the name in the method that is being overridden.

```
✗  public abstract class SomeClass
   {
       public abstract void SomeMethod(int parameter1);
   }

   public class SomeClassDerived : SomeClass
   {
       public override void SomeMethod(int parameter2)
       {
           // omitted
       }
   }
✓  public abstract class SomeClass
   {
       public abstract void SomeMethod(int parameter1);
   }

   public class SomeClassDerived : SomeClass
   {
       public override void SomeMethod(int parameter1)
       {
           // omitted
       }
   }
```

▸ Code Analysis CA1725

✻ A parameter **should not** use the Int64 (long) data type.

If code in a library is to be called by a Visual Basic 6 or VBA client such as Microsoft Office applications, they cannot create or pass Int64 (long) arguments.

⊗ If the library will never be called by Visual Basic 6 or VBA client, then Int64 arguments are permitted.

✻ A parameter used to select between two different values **should** have an enum data type, not a bool.

A parameter that selects between two different values that are not on/off, yes/no, or true/false should use an enum to select between them, not a bool. For example, to have the parameter to select between two different colors, use an enum to specify the color.

```
✗   /// <Summary>Sets the background color.</Summary>
    /// <param value="colorRed">
    /// Use true for red, false for blue
    /// </param>
    public void SetBackground(bool colorRed)
    {
        // omitted
    }

✓   public enum ImageBackgroundColor
    {
        Red,
        Blue
    }

    /// <Summary>Sets the background color.</Summary>
    /// <param value="imageBackgroundColor">
    ///     Specifies the background color.
    /// </param>
    public void SetBackground(
        ImageBackgroundColor imageBackgroundColor)
    {
        // omitted
    }
```

✱ A method that has an overload with a CultureInfo parameter
must be passed a CultureInfo.

The CultureInfo instructs .NET how to format the value in an
international setting. In most cases, this argument should be passed
CultureInfo.CurrentCulture.

```
✗   if (string.Compare("abc", "def", false) == 0)
    {
        // omitted
    }

✓   if (string.Compare(
        "abc",
        "def",
        false,
        CultureInfo.CurrentCulture) == 0))
    {
```

```
        // omitted
    }
```

▸ Code Analysis CA1304

✳ A method that has an overload with an **IFormatProvider** parameter **must** be passed an **IFormatProvider**.

The IFormatProvider instructs .NET how to format the value in an international setting. In most cases, this argument should be passed **CultureInfo.CurrentCulture**.

```
✗  string message = string.Format("{0}", 1);

✓  string message =
        string.Format(CultureInfo.CurrentCulture, "{0}", 1);
```

▸ Code Analysis CA1305

✳ A method that has an overload with a **StringComparison** parameter **must** be passed a **StringComparison**.

```
✗  if (string.Compare("abc", "def", false) == 0)
    {
        // omitted
    }

✓  if (string.Compare(
        "abc",
        0,
        "def",
        0,
        3,
        StringComparison.CurrentCulture) == 0)
    {
        // omitted
    }
```

▸ Code Analysis CA1307

✳ A string literal **should not** be passed as a parameter.

A string literal should be localized and stored as a resource rather than being imbedded into the source code.

Code Analysis will catch this if one or more of these are true:

- The LocalizableAttribute attribute of the parameter or property is set to true.

- The parameter or property name contains Text, Message, or Caption.

- The name of the string parameter that is passed to a Console.Write or Console.WriteLine is either value or format.

```
✗  Console.WriteLine("Message");

✓  Console.WriteLine(Resources.Message);
```

▸ Code Analysis CA1303

✳ Unused parameters **should** be removed.

Parameters that are unused in the body of the method should be removed.

⊗ If a method must implement an interface or abstract class, it must have a specific signature. In those cases, it is permissible to have an unused parameter.

```
✗  public void SomeMethod(int value)
   {
   }
✓  public void SomeMethod()
   {
   }
✓  public void SomeMethod(int value)
   {
        Console.WriteLine(value);
   }
```

▸ Code Analysis CA1801

✳ Parameters **must** all appear on one line or each on a separate line.

Parameters must all appear on the same line as the name of the method, or there must be an opening parenthesis and each parameter must appear on a separate line.

```
✗  public void SomeMethod(
       int value1,
```

```
            int value2, int value3)
        {
            // omitted
        }

✓ public void SomeMethod(int value1, int value2, int value3)
        {
            // omitted
        }

✓ public void SomeMethod(
            int value1,
            int value2,
            int value3)
        {
            // omitted
        }
```

▶ StyleCop SA1117

✻ A parameter, other than the first one, **must not** span multiple lines.

A parameter must appear on a single line of code. If the parameter is too long to fit on a single line, it should be assigned to a variable and the variable passed in the call.

```
✗ Console.WriteLine(
        "{0}",
        value
        + 2);

✓ Console.WriteLine(
        "{0}",
        value + 2);

✓ int writeValue = value + 2;
    Console.WriteLine(
        "{0}",
        writeValue);
```

▶ StyleCop SA1118

* If a parameter list spans multiple lines, it **must** begin on the line after the opening parenthesis.

```
✗  public void SomeMethod(

       int value)
   {
       // omitted
   }
✓  public void SomeMethod(
       int value)
   {
       // omitted
   }
✗  public void SomeMethod(int value1,
       int value2)
   {
       // omitted
   }
✓  public void SomeMethod(
       int value1,
       int value2)
   {
       // omitted
   }
```

  ▸ StyleCop SA1114, SA1116

* A comma following a parameter **must** be on the same line.

```
✗  public void SomeMethod(
       int value1
       , int value2)
   {
       // omitted
   }
✓  public void SomeMethod(
       int value1,
       int value2)
   {
```

```
      // omitted
  }
```

▸ StyleCop SA1113

✳ The opening parenthesis of a parameter list **must** appear on the same line as the declaration.

```
✗ Console.WriteLine
      ();

✔ Console.WriteLine();
```

▸ StyleCop SA1110

✳ The closing parenthesis of a parameter list **must** appear on the same line as the last parameter or the line of the opening parenthesis if there are no parameters.

```
✗ Console.WriteLine(
      1
      );

✔ Console.WriteLine(
      1);

✗ Console.WriteLine(
      );

✔ Console.WriteLine();
```

▸ StyleCop SA1111, SA1112

✳ A parameter **must** begin on the same line as a previous comma or the next line.

```
✗ public void SomeMethod(
      int value1,

      int value2)
  {
      // omitted
  }
```

```
✓  public void SomeMethod(
       int value1,
       int value2)
   {
       // omitted
   }
✓  public void SomeMethod(int value1, int value2)
   {
       // omitted
   }
```

▸ StyleCop SA1115

Preprocessor Directives

Preprocessor directives start with a # symbol. They are:

- #if
- #else
- #elif
- #endif
- #define
- #undef
- #warning
- #error
- #line
- #region
- #endregion
- #pragma
- #pragma warning
- #pragma checksum

✳ A conditional compilation symbol **must** use upper case.

Define conditional compilation symbols in the project properties build tab in Visual Studio using upper case and separated by semicolons. Visual Studio has checkboxes for the **DEBUG** and **TRACE** symbols. Each configuration may have different symbols defined. For example, the

Debug configuration may have the **DEBUG** symbol defined, whereas the Release configuration does not.

```
✗  #if debug
       // omitted
   #endif

✓  #if DEBUG
       // omitted
   #endif
```

✷ In a preprocessor directive, there **should** be no white space between the # symbol and the directive name.

The # symbol and the directive name should appear with no space between them.

```
✗  # if DEBUG
       // omitted
   #endif

✓  #if DEBUG
       // omitted
   #endif
```

▶ StyleCop SA1006

✷ Preprocessor directives **must not** be indented.

Preprocessor directives such as #if statements should be fully left justified.

```
✗  namespace SomeNamespace
   {
       public class SomeClass
       {
           public void SomeMethod()
           {
               #if DEBUG
               // omitted
               #endif
           }
       }
   }
```

```
✓ namespace SomeNamespace
  {
      public class SomeClass
      {
          public void SomeMethod()
          {
#if DEBUG
              // omitted
#endif
          }
      }
  }
```

✳ The contents of a preprocessor directive **should** be indented to the level the contents would use if the directive did not appear.

Avoid further indent the contents of preprocessor directives. Because preprocessor directives are fully left justified, only code that would normally appear in the first column will not be indented.

```
✗ [assembly: AssemblyCompany("Acme Corporation")]
  #if DEBUG
      [assembly: AssemblyConfiguration("Debug")]
  #else
      [assembly: AssemblyConfiguration("Release")]
  #endif
  [assembly: AssemblyCopyright("Copyright © 2020 Acme Corporation")]
✓ [assembly: AssemblyCompany("Acme Corporation")]
  #if DEBUG
  [assembly: AssemblyConfiguration("Debug")]
  #else
  [assembly: AssemblyConfiguration("Release")]
  #endif
  [assembly: AssemblyCopyright("Copyright © 2020 Acme Corporation")]
```

✳ Regions **must not** be used.

Regions obscure code, particularly when they are collapsed.

```
✗ #region SomeRegion
  // omitted
  #endregion
```

⊗ Regions may appear in automatically generated code that is not maintained by a programmer.

▸ StyleCop SA1109, SA1123, SA1124

Projects

✳ A project **must** include a CustomDictionary.xml file in the root of the project.

The CustomDictionary.xml file is described at https://msdn.microsoft.com/en-us/library/bb514188.aspx.

```
✓ <?xml version="1.0" encoding="utf-8"?>
  <Dictionary
      xmlns:xsi="http://www.w3.org/2001/XMLSchema-instance"
      xsi:noNamespaceSchemaLocation="CustomDictionary.xsd">
      <!--
          https://msdn.microsoft.com/en-us/library/bb514188.aspx
      -->
      <Acronyms>
          <CasingExceptions>
              <Acronym></Acronym>
          </CasingExceptions>
      </Acronyms>
      <Words>
          <Compound>
              <Term CompoundAlternate=""></Term>
          </Compound>
          <Deprecated>
              <Term PreferredAlternate=""></Term>
          </Deprecated>
          <DiscreteExceptions>
              <Term></Term>
          </DiscreteExceptions>
          <Recognized>
              <Word></Word>
          </Recognized>
          <Unrecognized>
              <Word></Word>
          </Unrecognized>
      </Words>
  </Dictionary>
```

The CustomDictionary.xml file can be a link to a common dictionary, shared by the solution, the group, or the company. The most common arrangement would be to include the real CustomDictionary.xml file in the root of the solution, then have each project in the solution link to it.

The **Acronym**, **Term** and **Word** elements of the file should be filled in by relevant words for the project. Sections of the XML that are not in use may be commented out.

The Build Action for the file must be set to **CodeAnalysisDictionary** in the file properties for it to be treated as a dictionary by Code Analysis.

▶ Code Analysis CA1701, CA1702, CA1703, CA1704, CA1709, CA1726, CA2204

✳ Warnings **should** always be set to warning level 4.

✳ Builds **should** use the "Microsoft All Rules" Code Analysis rule set.

⊗ If there are individual rules that an organization chooses to ignore, the Microsoft All Rules set should be modified to exclude just the ignored rules.

Properties

These related sections also apply to properties:

- Identifiers

- Scope

In the rules that follow, there is the concept of an externally visible side effect. A property with a side effect, in addition to returning a value, will also modify some state or has an observable interaction with calling functions or the outside world. For example, a property might modify a public, internal, or static field, write data to a display or file, read data, or call other side-effecting functions. In the presence of side effects, a program's behavior depends on history; that is, the order of evaluation matters.

Understanding a program with side effects requires knowledge about the context and its possible histories; and therefore can be hard to read, understand, and debug. Since a property is a reflection of the state of an object, setting or retrieving one should not cause visible side effects.

However, that does not mean that reading the property will not have an effect on state, as long as that state is not visible outside the type in which the property is defined. The most obvious example is that a property might cache some value that is expensive to retrieve.

✳ Properties **must** use Pascal case.

```
✗ public property count
  {
      get;
      set;
  }
✓ public property Count
  {
      get;
      set;
  }
```

▶ Code Analysis CA1709, StyleCop SA1300

✳ Setting or retrieving properties **should not** have externally visible side effects.

If setting or retrieving a property has a side effect, consider changing it to a method and prefixing it with the word Set or Get. For example, if there is a NextName property that passes back a different name from a database table on each request, that should be replaced by a "Get" method instead.

```
✗ /// <Summary>
  /// Gets next name from a database table.
  /// <Summary>
  public string NextName
  {
      // omitted
  }
✓ /// <Summary>
  /// Gets next name from a database table.
  /// <Summary>
  public string GetNextName()
  {
      // omitted
  }
```

If a property caches a result, that is not a violation of this rule, since the caching is not externally visible to the property.

✳ [Code Contracts] Properties that have no side effects **should** be decorated with the **Pure** attribute.

Only properties with the **Pure** attribute can be used in Code Contracts.

```
✗  public property Count
   {
       get;
       set;
   }
✓  [Pure]
   public property Count
   {
       get;
       set;
   }
```

✳ Properties **must not** be write-only.

Properties may be read-only or read-write, but not write-only. A write-only property should be replaced by a method. A property that can be set should also allow the value to be read, and should have no visible side effects.

```
✗  public bool WriteLine
   {
       set
       {
           // omitted
       }
   }
✓  public bool WriteLine(string value)
   {
       // omitted
   }
```

▶ Code Analysis CA1044

✳ If a property has both a **get** and **set** accessor, the **get** accessor **must** come first.

```
✗ public int SomeProperty
  {
      set
      {
          // omitted
      }

      get
      {
          // omitted
      }
  }
✓ public int SomeProperty
  {
      get
      {
          // omitted
      }

      set
      {
          // omitted
      }
  }
```

▸ StyleCop SA1212

✳ A private or internal property that is not called **should** be removed.

A private or internal property without a caller cannot be accessed from other places. The code should be removed or commented out.

⊗ The property can be left in if it will be used before the next public release.

✳ A read-only property **should** be used instead of a "Get" method.

Use a read-only property instead of a method if the method matches these criteria:

- The scope is public or protected.

- The method name is prefixed with the word "Get".

- The method has no parameters.

- The method returns a value that is not an array.

- The method is not computationally expensive each time it is called.

An example of a computationally expensive operation would be performing a lookup into a database each time the method is called. However, it is not considered computationally expensive if the value is retrieved from the database only once, and then cached for all further calls.

```
✗ public int GetIndex()
  {
      // omitted
  }

✓ public int Index
  {
      get
      {
          // omitted
      }
  }
```

▶ Code Analysis CA1024

✷ A property **should not** be named the same as a "Get" method.

A property should not have the same name as a method that begins with "Get". Remove or rename the method.

```
✗ public int Output
  {
      get
      {
          // omitted
      }
  }

  public int GetOutput()
  {
```

```
        // omitted
    }
✔ public int Output
    {
        get
        {
            // omitted
        }
    }
```

▶ Code Analysis CA1721

✳ A property **should not** return an array.

An array is not write protected, and can be changed after it is returned. To keep the array from being changed, a copy of the array will need to be generated. The caller will frequently be unaware of the cost of retrieving the property. Either change the property to be a method, or change the property to return a collection.

```
✘ public int[] SomeProperty
    {
        get
        {
            // omitted
        }
    }
✔ public ReadOnlyCollection<int> SomeProperty
    {
        get
        {
            // omitted
        }
    }
```

▶ Code Analysis CA1819

✳ Properties that represent a URI **must** be declared with the System.Uri class, not a string.

A property that represents a Uniform Resource Identifier (URI) should be declared with the System.Uri class, not a string. (See RFC 3305, https://tools.ietf.org/html/rfc3305 and related RFCs). A Uniform Resource Locator (URL) is a kind of URI. A string representation of a URI is liable to have parsing or encoding errors that lead to security vulnerabilities.

```
✗   public string Uri
    {
        get;
        set;
    }
✓   public Uri Uri
    {
        get;
        set;
    }
```

▸ Code Analysis CA1056

✳ Properties that do not reference the instance of a class **should** be marked static.

Properties that do not reference the instance of the class, usually via this, should be marked static. There is a distinct performance gain from not using instance members.

After marking a property as static, the compiler will emit nonvirtual calls to the property, which will prevent a check at runtime to make sure that the current object pointer is non-null. This can result in a measurable performance gain.

```
✗   public class SomeClass
    {
        public int SomeProperty
        {
            get
            {
                // Code that does not reference "this"
            }
        }
    }
✓   public class SomeClass
    {
        private static int someProperty;

        public static int SomeProperty
        {
```

```
            get
            {
                return someProperty;
            }
        }
    }
✓ public class SomeClass
    {
        private int someProperty;

        public static int SomeProperty
        {
            get
            {
                return this.someProperty;
            }
        }
    }
```

▸ Code Analysis CA1822

✳ Property Accessors **must** be written across multiple lines.

```
✗ public int SomeProperty
    {
        get { return this.someProperty; }
    }
✓ public int SomeProperty
    {
        get
        {
            return this.someProperty;
        }
    }
```

▸ StyleCop SA1504

References to Libraries

✳ A project **should not** include unused references.

If the code will still compile after a reference is removed, then that reference is unused. Unfortunately, there is currently no easy was to check for unused reference in Visual Studio.

Resources

✳ An unused resource **should** be removed.

Unused resources waste bytes in the executable.

✳ Resource names **should** be prefixed with an indicator of how the resource is to be used.

For example, prefix all resources that update a status bar message with StatusBar. This causes related resources to be grouped together.

Return Values

✳ The type of a return value of a public property or method **should not** be a List<T>.

List<T> is not designed to be inherited from. Instead of using List<T>, use Collection<T> instead

```
✗ public List<int> List
  {
      get
      {
          // omitted
      }
  }
✓ public Collection<int> List
  {
      get
      {
          // omitted
      }
  }
```

▸ Code Analysis CA1002

✳ The type of a return value of a property or method that represents a URI **should not** be a string.

The return value should be a System.Uri instead. If necessary, a ToString method can be performed on the return value.

```
✗ public string FindUri()
  {
      // omitted
  }
✓ public Uri FindUri()
  {
      // omitted
  }
```

▸ Code Analysis CA1055

Scope

✳ Elements **must** be given an access modifier defining the element's scope.

Even though elements have a default access modifier, they should be explicitly given.

```
✗ class SomeClass
  {
      void SomeMethod()
      {
          // omitted
      }
  }
✓ public class SomeClass
  {
      private void SomeMethod()
      {
          // omitted
      }
  }
```

▸ StyleCop SA1400

✳ Elements **should** be given the narrowest scope possible.

For most preferred to least preferred, the order of preference for scope is:

1. private
2. protected
3. internal
4. protected internal
5. public

An element should not be given the public access modifier if it can be given internal, for example.

⊗ An element's scope is determined by its final use, not necessarily the current minimum necessary to compile. For example, a method that will later need to be called by another internal component that has yet to be written should be given the internal access modifier, not private.

⊗ Give the entry point of the application the public access modifier, even if it could be given a more restricted one. For example, give the Main method of a console application the public access modifier.

✳ A private or internal member that is not used **must** be removed.

A private or internal member that is not used inside the assembly is dead code and must be removed or commented out.

▸ Code Analysis CA1811.

✳ The protected and protected internal scope **must not** be used in a sealed class or struct.

The protected scope is only useful when inheritance is allowed. A sealed class or struct cannot be inherited from, so using a protected scope must not be used.

```
✗  public sealed class SomeClass
   {
       protected void SomeMethod()
       {
           // omitted
       }
```

```
        // omitted
    }
✓ public sealed class SomeClass
    {
        private void SomeMethod()
        {
            // omitted
        }

        // omitted
    }
```

▶ Code Analysis CA1047

Structs

These related sections also apply to structs:

- Identifiers
- Scope
- Types

Structs use most of the same rules as classes.

Types

Types include classes, structs, enums, interfaces, and delegates. See these individual sections for more rules that apply to the specific kind of type.

✸ Types **should** be declared in namespaces.

All types should be declared inside a namespace.

```
✗ public class SomeClass
    {
        // omitted
    }
✓ namespace SomeNamespace
    {
        public class SomeClass
        {
            // omitted
```

```
    }
}
```

▶ Code Analysis CA1050

✳ A type name **must not** be named the same as the commonly used .NET Framework namespaces.

This is a list of the most commonly used namespaces from the .NET Framework. Do not name types (class, struct, delegate, enum, or interface) with these names.

- CodeAnalysis (System.Diagnostics.CodeAnalysis)
- Collections (System.Collections)
- CompilerServices (System.Runtime.CompilerServices)
- ComponentModel (System.ComponentModel)
- Contracts (System.Diagnostics.Contracts)
- Data (System.Data)
- Diagnostics (System.Diagnostics)
- Drawing (System.Drawing)
- Generic (System.Collections.Generic)
- Globalization (System.Globalization)
- InteropServices (System.Runtime.InteropServices)
- IO (System.IO)
- Linq (System.Linq)
- Reflection (System.Reflection)
- Serialization (System.Runtime.Serialization)
- System (System)
- Text (System.Text)
- Threading (System.Threading)
- ▶ Code Analysis CA1724

✳ Nested types **should not** be externally visible.

An externally visible type should not contain another externally visible type declaration. Either change the nested type to not be public, or make it so it is not nested.

⊗ Externally visible nested enums are permitted.

```
✗ public class SomeClass
  {
      // omitted

      public class NestedClass
      {
          // omitted
      }
  }
✓ public class SomeClass
  {
      // omitted

      private class NestedClass
      {
          // omitted
      }
  }
```

▸ Code Analysis CA1034

Using Directives

✳ Using directives **must** appear within the namespace.

The reasoning for this is that if more than one namespace appears in the file, the using directives are scoped to the namespace. Placing more than one namespace in the same file would violate other rules, but in unusual circumstances may occur. The Visual Studio templates do not follow this rule, so frequently code must be modified after the template code is added.

```
✗ using System;

  namespace SomeNamespace
  {
      // omitted
  }
✓ namespace SomeNamespace
  {
      using System;
```

```
      // omitted
  }
```

▸ StyleCop SA1200

✴ System using directives **must** appear before other using directives.

There is a Visual Studio option that will make the sorting of using directives place the System directives first. In Visual Studio, use the option Text Editor ⇨ C# ⇨ Advanced, and check the checkbox for "Place 'System' directives first when sorting usings".

```
✗ using Microsoft.CSharp;
  using System;

✓ using System;
  using Microsoft.CSharp;
```

▸ StyleCop SA1208

✴ Using directives **must** be ordered alphabetically.

System using directives must come first, then other using directives, then aliased using directives. However, within each group, they must be sorted alphabetically. Each part of the namespace separated by the periods is sorted separately.

```
✗ using System.Diagnostics;
  using System.Data;

✓ using System.Data;
  using System.Diagnostics;
```

▸ StyleCop SA1210

✴ Alias using directives **must** appear after all other using directives.

```
✗ using Alias = Microsoft.CSharp;
  using Microsoft.Win32;

✓ using Microsoft.Win32;
  using Alias = Microsoft.CSharp;
```

▸ StyleCop SA1209

✳ Alias using directives **must** be ordered alphabetically by alias name.

```
✗ using Foo = System.Data;
  using Bar = System.Diagnostics;

✓ using Bar = System.Diagnostics;
  using Foo = System.Data;
```

▸ StyleCop SA1211

✳ Unused using directives **must not** be present.

Right click on the using directives in Visual Studio and select Organize Usings ⇨ Remove and Sort.

✳ Using directives **should** be used, not fully qualified type names.

⊗ There are times that two libraries both in use have conflicting type names. In those cases, a fully qualified type name or a using directive alias should be used to distinguish between the classes.

```
✗ System.Collections.ObjectModel.Collection<int> collection =
      new System.Collections.ObjectModel.Collection<int>();

✓ using System.Collections.ObjectModel;
  // omitted
  Collection<int> collection = new Collection<int>();
```

Variables

These related sections also apply to variables:

- Identifiers
- Scope

✳ Unused local variables **must** be removed.

Local variables that are no longer being used must be removed or commented out.

▸ Code Analysis CA1804

✳ Excessive numbers of local variables **should** be avoided.

Local variables are stored in CPU registers for performance reasons. Excessive numbers of local variables cannot be mapped one-to-one with registers. If more than 64 local variables are used inside a method or property, it is probably a candidate for refactoring.

▶ Code Analysis CA1809

✳ A variable or parameter name **should not** match a field name.

A variable with the same name as a field makes code difficult to understand.

```
✗ public class SomeClass
  {
      private int someField;

      private void SomeMethod(int someField)
      {
          // omitted
      }
  }
✓ public class SomeClass
  {
      private int someField;

      private void SomeMethod(int someParameter)
      {
          // omitted
      }
  }
```

▶ Code Analysis CA1500

✳ Each variable **must** be defined on a separate line.

```
✗ int a, b = 1;
✓ int a;
  int b = 1;
```

✳ A variable that is returned from a method **should** be named result.

The default name for a variable that is returned from a method should be named result.

⊗ There may be times that another variable name makes the code easier to read. In those cases, another variable name may be used.

```
✔ public int Power(int x, int y)
  {
      int result = 0;
      if (y != 0)
      {
          result = (int)Math.Pow(x, y);
      }

      return result;
  }
```

✳ A variable **may** be named the same as its type, except in camel case.

The default name for a variable is frequently the name of its type, except in camel case instead of Pascal case.

```
✔ ReadOnlyCollection<int> readOnlyCollection;
```

⊗ There are many exceptions to this rule. When there are two variables of the same type in the same scope, they must be named differently. The variable that is returned from a method should be named result. In addition, it may make far more sense to give it some other name more related to what the variable represents. Therefore, this is a very loose guideline. It is used frequently in generic code, and less so in other places.

```
✔ ReadOnlyCollection<int> sizes;
```

XML Comments

These related sections also apply to XML comments:

• Comments

In the examples in this section, the example XML comments are merely meant to be placeholders for a more extensive comment. Most comments will be at least a full sentence, and some may run for several pages to fully document the item.

✴ An XML comment **must** be valid XML.

XML Comments must follow the XML specification (https://www.w3.org/TR/2006/REC-xml11-20060816). The most common violation of this rule is a missing closing tag.

```
✗  /// <summary>A description of SomeClass.
   public class SomeClass
   {
       // omitted
   }
✓  /// <summary>A description of SomeClass.</summary>
   public class SomeClass
   {
       // omitted
   }
```

▸ StyleCop SA1603

✴ Every element **must** be given XML comment documentation.

This includes enum values.

```
✗  public void SomeMethod()
   {
       // omitted
   }
✓  /// <summary>A description of SomeMethod.</summary>
   public void SomeMethod()
   {
       // omitted
   }
```

▸ StyleCop SA1600, SA1601, SA1602

✴ Every XML comment header **must** include a **<summary>** tag.

```
✗  /// <content>A description of SomeClass.</content>
   public class SomeClass
   {
```

```
        // omitted
    }

✓  /// <summary>A description of SomeClass.</summary>
    public class SomeClass
    {
        // omitted
    }
```

▸ StyleCop SA1604, SA1605

✳ An XML comment tag **must not** be blank.

Any XML comment tag that is present must contain a value. There must be text inside the tag. Thus, a self-closing XML comment tag is prohibited (for example **<summary />**), as well as tag that is empty or only contains white space.

```
✗  /// <summary></summary>
    public void SomeMethod()
    {
        // omitted
    }

✓  /// <summary>A description of SomeMethod.</summary>
    public void SomeMethod()
    {
        // omitted
    }
```

▸ StyleCop SA1606, SA1607, SA1610, SA1614, SA1616, SA1622, SA1627

✳ The XML comment **<summary>** tag **must** be changed from the Visual Studio default.

Visual Studio will sometimes help create an XML comment. The comment must be changed.

```
✗  /// <summary>Summary description for the SomeClass class.</summary>
    public class SomeClass
    {
        // omitted
    }
```

```
✔ /// <summary>Some other description of the SomeClass
   class.</summary>
   public class SomeClass
   {
       // omitted
   }
```

- ▶ StyleCop SA1608

✱ The **///** characters in an XML comment **must** be followed by a single space.

```
✗ ///<summary>omitted</summary>

✗ ///      <summary>omitted</summary>

✔ /// <summary>omitted</summary>
```

- ▶ StyleCop SA1004

✱ An XML comment header **must** be preceded by a blank line.

```
✗ /// <summary>The someField1 description.</summary>
   private int someField1 = 0;
   /// <summary>The someField1 description.</summary>
   private int someField2 = 0;

✔ /// <summary>The someField1 description.</summary>
   private int someField1 = 0;

   /// <summary>The someField1 description.</summary>
   private int someField2 = 0;
```

- ▶ StyleCop SA1514

✱ An XML comment header **must not** be followed by a blank line.

```
✗ /// <summary>A description of the SomeClass class.</summary>

   public class SomeClass
   {
       // omitted
   }
```

```
✓ /// <summary>A description of the SomeClass class.</summary>
   public class SomeClass
   {
       // omitted
   }
```

▸ StyleCop SA1506

✱ An XML comment header must not contain blank lines.

```
✗ /// <summary>
   ///
   /// A description of SomeMethod.
   ///
   /// </summary>
   public void SomeMethod()
   {
       // omitted
   }

✓ /// <summary>
   /// A description of SomeMethod.
   /// </summary>
   public void SomeMethod()
   {
       // omitted
   }
```

▸ StyleCop SA1644

✱ An XML comment header describing a property must have a value tag.

```
✗ /// <summary>Gets or sets SomeProperty.</summary>
   public int SomeProperty
   {
       get;
       set;
   }

✓ /// <summary>Gets or sets SomeProperty.</summary>
   /// <value>A description of the value.</value>
   public int SomeProperty
   {
```

```
        get;
        set;
    }
```

▸ StyleCop SA1609

✳ An XML <summary> tag for a property **must** have the proper description.

If the property is read-only, the <summary> tag must begin with the text "Gets". If the property has both get and set accessors and the set accessor is accessible, the <summary> tag must begin with text "Gets or sets". If the property has both get and set accessors and the set accessor has a more restricted scope than the property, the <summary> tag should begin with just "Gets".

```
✗  /// <summary>Gets SomeProperty.</summary>
   /// <value>A description of the value.</value>
   public int SomeProperty
   {
       get;
       set;
   }

✗  /// <summary>Gets SomeProperty.</summary>
   /// <value>A description of the value.</value>
   public int SomeProperty
   {
       get
       {
           // omitted
       }
   }

✓  /// <summary>Gets or sets SomeProperty.</summary>
   /// <value>A description of the value.</value>
   public int SomeProperty
   {
       get;
       set;
   }

✓  /// <summary>Gets SomeProperty.</summary>
   /// <value>A description of the value.</value>
   public int SomeProperty
```

```
    {
        get;
        private set;
    }
```

▸ StyleCop SA1623, SA1624

✻ An XML **<summary>** tag for a constructor **must** have the proper description.

The <summary> tag text for a constructor must begin with specific text. For a non-private instance constructor, the text should be "Initializes a new instance of the SomeClass class." For a static constructor, the text should be "Initializes static members of the SomeClass class." For generic classes, the type parameter should be included with the class name. Other tags can be embedded as part of the text, particularly a <see> tag.

```
✗ /// <summary>
  /// Creates a new instance of the SomeClass class.
  /// </summary>
  public SomeClass()
  {
      // omitted
  }

✓ /// <summary>
  /// Initializes a new instance of the SomeClass class.
  /// </summary>
  public SomeClass()
  {
      // omitted
  }

✓ /// <summary>
  /// Initializes static members of the SomeClass class.
  /// </summary>
  static SomeClass()
  {
      // omitted
  }

✓ /// <summary>
  /// Creates a new instance of the SomeClass<T> class.
  /// </summary>
```

```
    public SomeClass()
    {
        // omitted
    }
```

✓ ```
    /// <summary>
    /// Initializes a new instance of the <see cref="SomeClass"/>
    /// class.
    /// </summary>
    public SomeClass()
    {
        // omitted
    }
```

▸ StyleCop SA1642

✳ **An XML <summary> tag for a destructor must have the proper description.**

The <summary> tag text for a destructor must begin with specific text. The text should be "Finalizes an instance of the *ClassName* class." Other tags can be embedded as part of the text, particularly a <see> tag.

✗ ```
    /// <summary>
    /// Destructs an instance of the SomeClass class.
    /// </summary>
    ~SomeClass()
    {
        // omitted
    }
```

✓ ```
    /// <summary>
    /// Finalizes an instance of the SomeClass class.
    /// </summary>
    ~SomeClass()
    {
        // omitted
    }
```

✓ ```
    /// <summary>
    /// Finalizes an instance of the <see cref="SomeClass"/> class.
    /// </summary>
    ~SomeClass()
    {
```

```
        // omitted
    }
```

- ▸ StyleCop SA1643

✳ Element parameters **must** be documented in XML comments.

```
✗ /// <summary>Describes SomeMethod.</summary>
   public void SomeMethod(int value)
   {
       // omitted
   }

✓ /// <summary>Describes SomeMethod.</summary>
   /// <param name="value">Describes what value is for.</param>
   public void SomeMethod(int value)
   {
       // omitted
   }
```

- ▸ StyleCop SA1611

✳ In XML comments, element **<param>** tags **must** match the parameters.

A <param> tag must not appear in XML comments that is not in the actual code.

```
✗ /// <summary>Describes SomeMethod.</summary>
   /// <param name="item">Describes what value is for.</param>
   public void SomeMethod(int value)
   {
       // omitted
   }

✓ /// <summary>Describes SomeMethod.</summary>
   /// <param name="value">Describes what value is for.</param>
   public void SomeMethod(int value)
   {
       // omitted
   }
```

- ▸ StyleCop SA1612

✸ An XML comment **<param>** tag **must** have a name attribute.

```
✗  /// <summary>Describes SomeMethod.</summary>
   /// <param>Describes what value is for.</param>
   public void SomeMethod(int value)
   {
       // omitted
   }

✓  /// <summary>Describes SomeMethod.</summary>
   /// <param name="value">Describes what value is for.</param>
   public void SomeMethod(int value)
   {
       // omitted
   }
```

▶ StyleCop SA1613

✸ An element's return value **must** be documented in XML comments.

If an element returns a value, it must have a **<returns>** tag that describes the returned value.

```
✗  /// <summary>Describes SomeMethod.</summary>
   public int SomeMethod()
   {
       return 1;
   }

✓  /// <summary>Describes SomeMethod.</summary>
   /// <returns>The value 1.</returns>
   public int SomeMethod()
   {
       return 1;
   }
```

▶ StyleCop SA1615

✸ A void return value **must not** be documented.

```
✗  /// <summary>Describes SomeMethod.</summary>
   /// <returns>Returns nothing.</returns>
   public void SomeMethod()
   {
```

```
        // omitted
    }

✓   /// <summary>Describes SomeMethod.</summary>
    public void SomeMethod()
    {
        // omitted
    }
```

▸ StyleCop SA1617

✳ A generic type parameter **must** be documented in XML comments.

```
✗   /// <summary>Describes SomeMethod.</summary>
    public void SomeMethod<T>(T value)
    {
        // omitted
    }

✓   /// <summary>Describes SomeMethod.</summary>
    /// <typeparam name="T">Generic type parameter.</typeparam>
    /// <param name="value">The value being passed in.</param>
    public void SomeMethod<T>(T value)
    {
        // omitted
    }
```

▸ StyleCop SA1618, SA1619

✳ In XML comments, a generic type parameter **must** match the actual code.

```
✗   /// <summary>Describes SomeMethod.</summary>
    /// <typeparam name="Q">Generic type parameter.</typeparam>
    /// <param name="value">The value being passed in.</param>
    public void SomeMethod<T>(T value)
    {
        // omitted
    }

✓   /// <summary>Describes SomeMethod.</summary>
    /// <typeparam name="T">Generic type parameter.</typeparam>
    /// <param name="value">The value being passed in.</param>
    public void SomeMethod<T>(T value)
```

```
    {
        // omitted
    }
```

▸ StyleCop SA1620

✱ An XML comment **<typeparam>** tag **must** have a name attribute.

```
✗ /// <summary>Describes SomeMethod.</summary>
   /// <typeparam>Generic type parameter.</typeparam>
   /// <param name="value">The value being passed in.</param>
   public void SomeMethod<T>(T value)
   {
       // omitted
   }

✓ /// <summary>Describes SomeMethod.</summary>
   /// <typeparam name="T">Generic type parameter.</typeparam>
   /// <param name="value">The value being passed in.</param>
   public void SomeMethod<T>(T value)
   {
       // omitted
   }
```

▸ StyleCop SA1621

✱ An XML comment description **should not** be identical to another description in the same XML comment header.

This most often means that the comment was copied and pasted without reviewing its contents.

```
✗ /// <summary>Describes SomeMethod.</summary>
   /// <param name="value1">An identical description.</param>
   /// <param name="value2">An identical description.</param>
   public void SomeMethod(int value1, int value2)
   {
       // omitted
   }

✓ /// <summary>Describes SomeMethod.</summary>
   /// <param name="value1">A description of value1.</param>
   /// <param name="value2">A description of value2.</param>
   public void SomeMethod(int value1, int value2)
```

```
    {
        // omitted
    }
```

▸ StyleCop SA1625

✳ XML comment documentation text **must** begin with a capital letter.

```
✗ /// <summary>describes SomeMethod.</summary>
   public void SomeMethod()
   {
       // omitted
   }

✓ /// <summary>Describes SomeMethod.</summary>
   public void SomeMethod()
   {
       // omitted
   }
```

▸ StyleCop SA1628

✳ XML comment documentation text **must** end with a period.

Note: The current version of StyleCop is not very forgiving about this rule. It gives a warning if there is a phrase enclose in parentheses at the end of the documentation text. This should be allowed as long as the phrase ends in a period.

```
✗ /// <summary>Describes SomeMethod</summary>
   public void SomeMethod()
   {
       // omitted
   }

✓ /// <summary>Describes SomeMethod.</summary>
   public void SomeMethod()
   {
       // omitted
   }
```

▸ StyleCop SA1629

✳ XML documentation text **must** be spelled correctly.

```
✗   /// <summary>Describes SoomeMethod.</summary>
    public void SomeMethod()
    {
        // omitted
    }

✓   /// <summary>Describes SomeMethod.</summary>
    public void SomeMethod()
    {
        // omitted
    }
```

▸ StyleCop SA1650

✳ An include file reference **must** have valid file and path
   attributes.

```
✗   /// <summary>Some Class.</summary>
    /// <include path="//member[@name='RuleSA1647']" />
    public class SomeClass
    {
        // omitted
    }

✗   /// <summary>Some Class.</summary>
    /// <include file="Documentation.xml" />
    public class SomeClass
    {
        // omitted
    }

✓   /// <summary>Some Class.</summary>
    /// <include file="Documentation.xml"
    /// path="//member[@name='RuleSA1647']" />
    public class SomeClass
    {
        // omitted
    }
```

▸ StyleCop SA1647

❉ An include file reference in an XML comment **must** refer to an existing file.

```
✗ /// <summary>Some method. NoFile.xml does not exist.</summary>
  /// <include file="NoFile.xml" path="//member[@name='RuleSA1645']"
  />
  public static void SomeMethod()
  {
      // omitted
  }

✓ /// <summary>Some method. SomeFile.xml exists.</summary>
  /// <include file="SomeFile.xml"
  path="//member[@name='RuleSA1645']" />
  public static void SomeMethod()
  {
      // omitted
  }
```

▶ StyleCop SA1645

❉ An include file reference in an XML comment **must** refer to a path that exists.

```
✗ /// <summary>Some method. NoRuleSA1646 does not exists.</summary>
  /// <include file="Documentation.xml"
  /// path="//member[@name='NoRuleSA1646']" />
  public static void SomeMethod()
  {
      // omitted
  }

✓ /// <summary>Some method. RuleSA1646 exists.</summary>
  /// <include file="Documentation.xml"
  /// path="//member[@name='RuleSA1646']" />
  public static void SomeMethod()
  {
      // omitted
  }
```

▶ StyleCop SA1646

✳ An inheritdoc element in an XML comment **must** be used on a member that inherits from another class.

An inheritdoc element causes the documentation to be inherited from the base class. If there is no base class, then there is no documentation to inherit.

```
✗  public class SomeClass
   {
       /// <inheritdoc />
       public override void SomeMethod()
       {
           Console.WriteLine(this);
       }
   }

✓  public class SomeBaseClass
   {
       /// <summary>Some Method.</summary>
       public virtual void SomeMethod()
       {
           Console.WriteLine(this);
       }
   }

   public class SomeClass : SomeBaseClass
   {
       /// <inheritdoc />
       public override void SomeMethod()
       {
           Console.WriteLine(this);
       }
   }
```

▶ StyleCop SA1648

PROJECT MANAGEMENT BEST PRACTICES

Compiler Warnings and Errors

✳ The option to "Enable Code Analysis on Build" **should** be turned on in the project properties.

Problems with code should be fixed immediately. If the build performance is too slow, this can be turned off; however, Code Analysis must be run before a check-in.

✳ All compiler warnings **must** be fixed or suppressed before check-in.

✳ Code Analysis and StyleCop **should** be used before check-in.

✳ All Code Analysis and StyleCop warnings **should** be fixed or suppressed.

If necessary, warnings may be suppressed after careful review. Team policy may be that all suppressed warnings are reviewed by a team lead or other team member.

✳ Suppressed warnings **must** be given a justification.

▸ StyleCop SA1404

Public Releases

The process of making releases differs from organization to organization, but some generalities can be stated here.

Microsoft has a document called *Code Signing Best Practices* that details many issues to think about on signing code and making releases. It can be downloaded from http://www.microsoft.com/whdc/winlogo/drvsign/best_practices.mspx.

＊ There **should** be a person in charge of making releases.

This person is responsible for making the releases correctly. This needs to be a responsible person, trusted within the company. If the organization releases code with a Trojan embedded into it, or allows the company private key to escape so that a Trojan can be inserted later without detection, the results can be disastrous.

＊ There **should** be a checklist to follow in making a release.

This list will be different from company to company, but should detail all of the steps in making a release.

＊ Released code **may** be checked to see if references can be removed.

There is no easy way to see if a reference can be removed. The easiest way is to make sure that code compiles, then remove the reference and see if it still compiles. If so, then the reference is unused. If it no longer compiles, the reference must be re-added. This is tedious if there are many references. However, this should be done on the first release and periodically thereafter, if not on every release.

＊ Releases **should** be signed with a different strong name private key than the one used for development.

This key must be tightly controlled so that it does not wind up in untrusted hands.

＊ Releases **must** be virus scanned before releasing to the customer.

The latest updates should be downloaded before the scan.

＊ Verify that the version number has increased since the last release.

＊ All commented out code **should** be reviewed.

All code that begins with //// should be reviewed and in most cases removed. Any code that remains should be prefixed with a comment describing why it is being retained.

```
✔ ////// Reviewed 2020-06-29. Will be reinstated in Release 2.2
  ////// after the new version of the PortableHole library is
```

```
////// released.
////public void SomeMethod()
////{
////    // omitted
////}
```

★ There **must** be no comments remaining in the code that begin with TODO or UNDONE.

Comments with TODO or UNDONE in them should be reviewed. Any that are postponed should be removed and a work item created in the project management software for the next release.

⊗ Alpha releases may still have uncompleted work items in them.

Directories

★ Solutions **should** be stored subdirectories of the \src directory in the root of a drive on the local computer.

This makes it so that there is a standard place to look on a local computer for the sources. This is useful if someone breaks a build or forgets to check in a file, the projects can be quickly located on their computer.

```
✗  c:\projects\Acme\Acme.PortableHoleGenerator
✓  c:\src\Acme\Acme.PortableHoleGenerator
```

⊗ A group may standardize on any other location on the disk. The \src directory may be on any drive on the computer.

SECURITY BEST PRACTICES

＊ The strong name key (.snk) file used to sign public releases **should not** be checked into the version control system for a project.

A strong name on an assembly is one part of a security scheme. By itself, it does not secure the files it is used to sign. Access to strong name key would allow silent changes to a released file. Since generally many people have access to the source code of a project, allowing them all to have the .snk file used for releases can allow a security breach.

The recommended practice is that there should be at least two separate .snk files. They are:

- The .snk used for public releases (the release key)

- The .snk used for development and internal releases (the development key)

There may be other keys used for special builds, such as beta releases.

The release key should be a carefully controlled file, with only a limited number of employees having access to it, and the security of the file as tightly controlled as if it were a pile of cash. If this key gets into the wild, then all past releases that used it are suspect, and the key should be retired from use for future builds.

If the directory for a solution is c:\src\Solution, then the .snk file should be placed into the c:\src directory, which is not part of the project sources checked into source control. When signing project for the first time, Visual Studio will copy the .snk file into the project. However, what is needed is a link to a the file. This can be accomplished by editing the project file.

Close the solution, and then edit the project file inside a text editor. Find and replace the .snk file name with ..\..\filename.snk inside the project file, with enough parent directory redirections from the project file to the location of the .snk file. Delete the file from the project. Then check the project into the source control. This will keep the .snk file from being part of the project or accidentally being checked in.

If the release key is ever checked into the project, it is difficult to erase all records of the file, because the object of version control is to maintain all changes. There are ways of permanently forgetting the file (for example, the "destroy" command on Team Foundation Server), but during the time it was checked in, it may have been leaked.

The development key may be checked into the version control, but not referenced by the project at that location. The development key file should be copied to the appropriate directory before the code can be compiled. In the example above, this would be copied to the c:\src directory.

✳ A process **should** be established that will be implemented if a release key ever becomes compromised.

This may involve notifying clients, re-signing previous builds, or making new releases with a new key, among other steps.

APPENDIX A
PROHIBITED IDENTIFIER NAMES

These keywords should not be used for public identifier names. They are common keywords of the most popular .NET languages. Their use will make it difficult to use a library across languages. Do not use any capitalization of these keywords.

AddHandler	AddressOf	Alias	And
Ansi	As	Assembly	Auto
Base	Boolean	ByRef	Byte
ByVal	Call	Case	Catch
CBool	CByte	CChar	CDate
CDbl	CDec	Char	CInt
Class	CLng	CObj	Const
CShort	CSng	CStr	CType
Date	Decimal	Declare	Default
Delegate	Dim	Do	Double
Each	Else	ElseIf	End
Enum	Erase	Error	Eval
Event	Exit	Extends	ExternalSource
False	Finalize	Finally	Float
For	Friend	Function	Get
GetType	Goto	Handles	If
Implements	Imports	In	Inherits
InstanceOf	Integer	Interface	Is
Let	Lib	Like	Long
Loop	Me	Mod	Module
MustInherit	MustOverride	MyBase	MyClass
Namespace	New	Next	Not
Nothing	NotInheritable	NotOverridable	Object
On	Option	Optional	Or
Overloads	Overridable	Overrides	Package
ParamArray	Preserve	Private	Property
Protected	Public	RaiseEvent	ReadOnly

ReDim	Region	Rem	RemoveHandler
Resume	Return	Select	Set
Shadows	Shared	Short	Single
Static	Step	Stop	String
Structure	Sub	SyncLock	Then
Throw	To	True	Try
TypeOf	Unicode	Until	Var
Volatile	When	While	With
WithEvents	WriteOnly	Xor	

APPENDIX B
SUFFIXES FOR CERTAIN TYPES

The suffixes listed below should always be used for the type listed. In addition, a type should never end in the suffix listed unless it is of the type listed.

Base Type or Interface	Suffix
An event handler delegate	EventHandler
Attribute	Attribute
DataSet	DataSet or Collection
DataTable	DataTable or Collection
EventArgs	EventArgs
Exception	Exception
ICollection	Collection
IDictionary	Dictionary
IEnumerable	Collection
IMembershipCondition	Condition
IPermission	Permission
Queue	Queue or Collection
Stack	Stack or Collection
Stream	Stream

APPENDIX C
CHECKLIST FOR BEST
PRACTICES

✳ Establish a committee for deciding on Best Practices.

All changes to the Best Practices should be agreed on by the committee. The changes should be documented for review and posterity.

✳ Establish where variations from these Best Practices will be documented.

These variations should be available to the entire programming team. An internal web site or wiki is an appropriate place for such documentation.

✳ Establish a procedure for justifying Code Analysis and StyleCop rule suppressions.

Decide on how rule suppressions should be reviewed and allowed. A few of common schemes:

- A review committee
- A development lead
- Peer review

✳ Decide whether goto statements require code review, and if so by what process.

It may be that different levels of programmers require different levels of review.

* Check with legal counsel for the correct form of copyright and trademark notices for the project.

   Determine when copyright notices should be changed as well. For example, on a web site, they may be changed on the first business day of the year.

* Establish a process building releases and maintaining the release key used to sign public releases.

   An example is that public releases are built on a secure machine in a locked room by the project lead. Various systems record access to the machine. The key used to sign the public releases is only on that machine and a backup in a safe deposit box. That machine is never exposed on the company network and never used for anything except building releases.

* Establish a checklist for the process for making a public release.

   There may be different checklists for different kinds of releases: Alpha, Beta, shipping releases, publishing to an internal web site, publishing to an Internet facing web site, and so forth. The list or lists should determine who does what when, and what sort of signoff is necessary for each step.

* Establish a process that will be executed if a release strong name key ever become compromised.

* Decide what version control system will be used

   Choose between Team Foundation Server, Git, and Subversion or some other system, and where to host the sources. Choose who will have access and what privileges they will have.

* Decide whether code will be required to have unit tests.

   If tests are required, then what policies should be required for the unit tests?

✳ Decide what policies need to be met before checking in code.

Decide whether unit tests must be written and run. Decide whether what warnings must be fixed or suppressed. Decide what code reviews must be performed.

✳ Decide whether to use Code Contracts.

If Code Contracts are used, will validation of parameters use Contract.Requires or legacy custom parameter validation with Contract.EndBlock?

✳ Decide how and when logging will be performed

Particularly decide how the handling unexpected exceptions will happen. Decide if NLog, Log4Net, or some other logging library will be used.

APPENDIX D
ALTERNATE CHOICES

This style guide is a suggestion not a prescription. Below is a list of topics that tend to be most controversial, and provides some alternate choices. It is more important to be consistent than the particular practices adopted.

This might be considered the starting agenda for a Best Practices Committee, and may need to be revisited on the creation of each new solution.

- Brace Style. The C# standard is to use the Allman style, but there are many other styles, particularly from programmers commonly using C or C++. Choose a brace style.

- Indenting. The standard presented here is to perform indenting with tabs. However, many groups choose to use spaces instead.

- Fields. The standard presented here is to use no special prefix for fields, but prefix all references to references to fields with this. However many groups prefix fields with an underscore or m_.

- XML Comments. The standard presented here is that all elements should have XML Comments. However, some teams only require that public elements need XML Comments. Some do not use them at all. Decide what code will use XML comments.

- Internationalization. Decide how much support will be given to internationalization, and whether all strings should be moved into resource files rather than being hard coded.

- Use of var. The standard presented here is to use var for variable and field declarations as little as possible. However, some groups use var as much as possible.

- Sorting code. The standard presented here is that all code must appear in a particular order inside a file. However, this does make tracking code changes in a version control system more difficult when the refactoring code, since the location in the file must change when scope or name changes. Decide whether code should be sorted.

- Line Length. Choose a maximum line length for code. The standard presented here is 140 characters per line.

- Regions. The standard presented here is to disallow regions. Decide whether regions are permitted.

- The directory where source code is stored. The standard presented here is to store source code in a subdirectory of the \src directory. Choose a location to store code.

- Code Analysis Rules sets. The standard presented here is to use the "Microsoft All Rules" rules set. Decide what Code Analysis rules set or sets to use, or create a custom set to use.

All other rules may also be changed, but these are the most common.

APPENDIX E
EXAMPLE CODE

The next several pages show example code using the rules presented here. This code generates the cover for the print version of this book and places it into a PDF file. It uses a NuGet package called PDFSharp to create the PDF file from the bitmap it creates for the cover. It also creates a separate JPG file for the cover of the Kindle version of the book. The code uses Code Contracts.

There are two projects in the solution: Xoc.CoverGenerator and Xoc.Penrose. Xoc.CoverGenerator is a console application that generates the cover. It calls Xoc.Penrose, that creates the background image on the cover using Penrose tiling. All of the details used to specify the cover are stored in the App.Config file.

The code does not use all the rules in the style guide, but does show a representative example of production quality code using the styles.

The code is written using C# version 6. The code is available at https://github.com/GregReddick/Xoc.CoverGenerator.

Xoc.CoverGenerator\Properties\AssemblyInfo.cs

```
//-----------------------------------------------------------------------
// <copyright file="AssemblyInfo.cs" company="Xoc Software">
// Copyright © 2015 Xoc Software
// </copyright>
// <summary>Implements the assembly information class</summary>
//-----------------------------------------------------------------------
using System;
using System.Diagnostics.Contracts;
using System.Reflection;
using System.Resources;
using System.Runtime.InteropServices;

[assembly: AssemblyCompany("Xoc Software")]
#if DEBUG
[assembly: AssemblyDelaySign(false)]
[assembly: AssemblyConfiguration("Debug")]
#else
[assembly: AssemblyConfiguration("Release")]
#endif
[assembly: AssemblyCopyright("Copyright © 2015 Xoc Software")]
[assembly: AssemblyDelaySign(false)]
[assembly: AssemblyDescription("Generates cover for the book.")]
[assembly: AssemblyInformationalVersion("1.0")]
[assembly: AssemblyProduct("Xoc.CoverGenerator")]
[assembly: AssemblyTitle("Xoc Cover Generator")]
[assembly: AssemblyTrademark("Xoc is a trademark of Xoc Software")]
[assembly: AssemblyVersion("1.0.*")]
[assembly: CLSCompliant(true)]
[assembly: ComVisible(false)]
[assembly: ContractVerification(true)]
[assembly: Guid("88b8a824-3272-4bf4-a0d4-f74a032b1b")]
[assembly: NeutralResourcesLanguage("en-US")]

/// <summary>Gives information about the assembly.</summary>
internal static class AssemblyInfo
{
    /// <summary>Gets an assembly attribute.</summary>
    /// <typeparam name="T">An assembly attribute type.</typeparam>
```

```csharp
    /// <returns>The assembly attribute of type T.</returns>
    internal static T Attribute<T>()
        where T : Attribute
    {
        return typeof(AssemblyInfo).Assembly.GetCustomAttribute<T>();
    }
}
```

Xoc.CoverGenerator\GraphicsExtensions.cs

```csharp
//------------------------------------------------------------------------------
// <copyright file="GraphicsExtensions.cs" company="Xoc Software">
// Copyright © 2015 Xoc Software
// </copyright>
// <summary>Implements the graphics extensions class</summary>
//------------------------------------------------------------------------------

namespace Xoc.CoverGenerator
{
    using System;
    using System.Diagnostics.Contracts;
    using System.Drawing;
    using System.Drawing.Drawing2D;
    using CoverGenerator.Properties;

    /// <summary>The graphics extensions.</summary>
    internal static class GraphicsExtensions
    {
        /// <summary>The Graphics extension method that draws an embossed string.</summary>
        /// <param name="graphics">The graphics object to act on.</param>
        /// <param name="s">The string to write.</param>
        /// <param name="font">The font to use.</param>
        /// <param name="brush">The brush for the color of the string.</param>
        /// <param name="point">The point that locates the string.</param>
        /// <param name="size">The size of the box (required).</param>
        internal static void DrawStringEmbossed(this Graphics graphics, string s, Font font, Brush brush, PointF point, SizeF size)
        {
            Contract.Requires<ArgumentNullException>(graphics != null);
            Contract.Requires<ArgumentNullException>(font != null);
```

217

```csharp
graphics.DrawStringEmbossed(
    s,
    font,
    brush,
    new RectangleF(point.X, point.Y, size.Width, size.Height),
    null);
}

/// <summary>The Graphics extension method that draws an embossed string.</summary>
/// <param name="graphics">The graphics object to act on.</param>
/// <param name="s">The string to write.</param>
/// <param name="font">The font to use.</param>
/// <param name="brush">The brush for the color of the string.</param>
/// <param name="layoutRectangle">The layout rectangle for the string.</param>
/// <param name="format">Describes the format to use.</param>
internal static void DrawStringEmbossed(
    this Graphics graphics,
    string s,
    Font font,
    Brush brush,
    RectangleF layoutRectangle,
    StringFormat format)
{
    Contract.Requires<ArgumentNullException>(graphics != null);
    Contract.Requires<ArgumentNullException>(font != null);

    using (Brush brushSmear = new SolidBrush(Color.FromArgb(96, Color.DarkRed)))
    {
        graphics.FillRoundedRectangle(brushSmear, layoutRectangle, 20);
    }

    RectangleF shadow = layoutRectangle;
    int offset = (int)(font.SizeInPoints <= 14 ? graphics.DpiX / 300 : graphics.DpiX / 100);
    shadow.Offset(offset, offset);
    graphics.DrawString(
        s,
        font,
        Brushes.Gray,
```

```csharp
                shadow,
                format);
            graphics.DrawString(
                s,
                font,
                brush,
                layoutRectangle,
                format);
        }

        /// <summary>The Graphics extension method that fills a rounded rectangle.</summary>
        /// <param name="graphics">The graphics to act on.</param>
        /// <param name="brush">The brush to draw.</param>
        /// <param name="layoutRectangle">The layout rectangle.</param>
        /// <param name="cornerRadius">The corner radius.</param>
        internal static void FillRoundedRectangle(this Graphics graphics, Brush brush, RectangleF layoutRectangle, int cornerRadius)
        {
            Contract.Requires<ArgumentNullException>(graphics != null);

            using (GraphicsPath graphicsPath = new GraphicsPath())
            {
                graphicsPath.AddArc(layoutRectangle.X, layoutRectangle.Y, cornerRadius, cornerRadius, 180, 90);
                graphicsPath.AddArc(
                    layoutRectangle.X + layoutRectangle.Width - cornerRadius,
                    layoutRectangle.Y,
                    cornerRadius,
                    cornerRadius,
                    270,
                    90);
                graphicsPath.AddArc(
                    layoutRectangle.X + layoutRectangle.Width - cornerRadius,
                    layoutRectangle.Y + layoutRectangle.Height - cornerRadius,
                    cornerRadius,
                    cornerRadius,
                    0,
                    90);
                graphicsPath.AddArc(
                    layoutRectangle.X,
```

```
            layoutRectangle.Y + layoutRectangle.Height - cornerRadius,
            cornerRadius,
            cornerRadius,
            90,
            90);

        graphicsPath.CloseAllFigures();
        graphics.FillPath(brush, graphicsPath);
      }
    }
  }
```

Xoc.CoverGenerator\PageType.cs

```
//-------------------------------------------------------------------
// <copyright file="PageType.cs" company="Xoc Software">
// Copyright © 2015 Xoc Software
// </copyright>
// <summary>Implements the page type enum</summary>
//-------------------------------------------------------------------
namespace Xoc.CoverGenerator
{
  using System;

  /// <summary>
  /// Values that represent the CreateSpace page types. Each entry here must have a corresponding entry in the switch
  /// statement in PageThickness.
  /// </summary>
  [Serializable]
  public enum PageType
  {
    /// <summary>White pages.</summary>
    White,

    /// <summary>Cream pages.</summary>
    Cream,

    /// <summary>Color pages.</summary>
    Color
```

```
        }

}

Xoc.CoverGenerator\Program.cs
//----------------------------------------------------------------
// <copyright file="Program.cs" company="Xoc Software">
// Copyright © 2015 Xoc Software
// </copyright>
// <summary>Implements the program class</summary>
//----------------------------------------------------------------
namespace Xoc.CoverGenerator
{
    using System;
    using System.Diagnostics;
    using System.Diagnostics.Contracts;
    using System.Drawing;
    using System.Drawing.Imaging;
    using System.Globalization;
    using System.IO;
    using System.Reflection;
    using System.Windows.Media.Imaging;
    using PdfSharp.Drawing;
    using PdfSharp.Pdf;
    using Penrose;
    using Properties;

    /// <summary>
    /// The program to draw the book cover. Draws to both a CreateSpace pdf and a Kindle file. These are brought up in the
    /// default viewers for the types and must be saved.
    /// </summary>
    internal static class Program
    {
        /// <summary>Gets the page thickness, which depends on the page type.</summary>
        /// <value>The page thickness in fractions of an inch.</value>
        private static float PageThicknessInches
        {
            get
            {
```

The Reddick C# Style Guide

```csharp
        float result;

        PageType pageType = Settings.Default.PageType;
        switch (pageType)
        {
            default:
            case PageType.White:
                result = Settings.Default.PageThicknessWhiteInches;
                break;
            case PageType.Cream:
                result = Settings.Default.PageThicknessCreamInches;
                break;
            case PageType.Color:
                result = Settings.Default.PageThicknessColorInches;
                break;
        }

        return result;
    }

    /// <summary>Main entry-point for the application.</summary>
    public static void Main()
    {
        try
        {
            Console.OutputEncoding = System.Text.Encoding.UTF8;
            Console.WriteLine(AssemblyInfo.Attribute<AssemblyTitleAttribute>()?.Title);
            Console.WriteLine(AssemblyInfo.Attribute<AssemblyCopyrightAttribute>()?.Copyright);

            int penroseIterations = Settings.Default.PenroseIterations;
            RhombusTiler rhombusTiler = new RhombusTiler(penroseIterations);

            SizeF sizeBookTrimInches = Settings.Default.SizeBookTrimInches;

            Program.MakeCreateSpaceCover(rhombusTiler, sizeBookTrimInches);
            Program.MakeKindleCover(rhombusTiler, sizeBookTrimInches);
        }
```

222

```csharp
catch (Exception ex)
{
    // Generic exception handling at the top of the call stack
    Console.WriteLine(Resources.ErrorMessage, ex.Message);
}
}

/// <summary>Adds a back cover text.</summary>
/// <param name="graphics">The graphics object to draw to.</param>
/// <param name="dpi">The DPI of the cover.</param>
/// <param name="rectSafe">The back cover safe rectangle.</param>
private static void AddBackCoverText(Graphics graphics, int dpi, RectangleF rectSafe)
{
    Contract.Requires<ArgumentNullException>(graphics != null);

    Font fontBlurb = null;

    try
    {
        float marginText = Settings.Default.MarginTextInches * dpi;
        string directoryImages = Settings.Default.DirectoryImages;
        Contract.Assume(directoryImages != null);

        // Draw the blurb
        string bookBlurb = Settings.Default.BookBlurb;
        PointF pointBlurb = new PointF(rectSafe.X + marginText, rectSafe.Y + marginText);
        fontBlurb = new Font(Settings.Default.FontTypeface, Settings.Default.FontBlurbSize);
        SizeF sizeTextBlurb = graphics.MeasureString(bookBlurb, fontBlurb, (int)Math.Ceiling(rectSafe.Width - (2 * marginText)));
        graphics.DrawStringEmbossed(bookBlurb, fontBlurb, Brushes.White, pointBlurb, sizeTextBlurb);

        // Draw the logo
        string logoFileNameFull = string.Format(CultureInfo.InvariantCulture, Settings.Default.FileNameLogo, dpi);
        Contract.Assume(logoFileNameFull != null);
        string logoPathName = Path.Combine(directoryImages, logoFileNameFull);
        if (File.Exists(logoPathName))
        {
            using (Bitmap bitmapLogo = new Bitmap(logoPathName))
            {
```

```
            graphics.DrawImage(bitmapLogo, rectSafe.X + marginText, rectSafe.Bottom - marginText - bitmapLogo.Height);
        }

        // Draw the ISBN
        SizeF sizeIsbnBlockInches = Settings.Default.SizeIsbnBlockInches;
        SizeF sizeIsbnBlock = new SizeF(sizeIsbnBlockInches.Width * dpi, sizeIsbnBlockInches.Height * dpi);
        RectangleF rectIsbn = new RectangleF(
            rectSafe.Right - marginText - sizeIsbnBlock.Width,
            rectSafe.Bottom - marginText - sizeIsbnBlock.Height,
            sizeIsbnBlock.Width,
            sizeIsbnBlock.Height);

        graphics.FillRectangle(Brushes.White, rectIsbn);

        if (Settings.Default.ShowIsbn)
        {
            // Get the isbn graphic and draw it on the back. If not done, CoverSpace will automatically add an ISBN barcode to the
            // white block.
            string isbnFileNameFull = string.Format(CultureInfo.InvariantCulture, Settings.Default.FileNameIsbn, dpi);
            Contract.Assume(isbnFileNameFull != null);
            string isbnPathName = Path.Combine(directoryImages, isbnFileNameFull);
            if (File.Exists(isbnPathName))
            {
                using (Bitmap bitmapIsbn = new Bitmap(isbnPathName))
                {
                    graphics.DrawImage(bitmapIsbn, rectIsbn.Left, rectIsbn.Top, rectIsbn.Width, rectIsbn.Height);
                }
            }
        }
    }
    finally
    {
        fontBlurb?.Dispose();
    }
}

/// <summary>Adds a front cover text.</summary>
```

```csharp
/// <param name="graphics">The graphics object to draw to.</param>
/// <param name="dpi">The DPI of the cover.</param>
/// <param name="rectSafe">The front cover safe rectangle.</param>
private static void AddFrontCoverText(Graphics graphics, int dpi, RectangleF rectSafe)
{
    Contract.Requires<ArgumentNullException>(graphics != null);

    Font fontTitle = null;
    Font fontAuthor = null;
    Font fontSubtitle = null;
    Font fontDraft = null;

    try
    {
        string fontTypeface = Settings.Default.FontTypeface;
        string bookTitle = Settings.Default.BookTitle;
        string bookAuthor = Settings.Default.BookAuthor;
        string bookSubtitle = Settings.Default.BookSubtitle;
        string bookDraftText = Settings.Default.BookDraftText;
        float spacingTitle = Settings.Default.SpacingTitleInches * dpi;
        float spacingAuthor = Settings.Default.SpacingAuthorInches * dpi;
        float spacingSubtitle = Settings.Default.SpacingSubtitleInches * dpi;
        float spacingDraft = Settings.Default.SpacingDraftInches * dpi;

        fontAuthor = new Font(fontTypeface, Settings.Default.FontAuthorSize);
        fontDraft = new Font(fontTypeface, Settings.Default.FontDraftSize);
        fontSubtitle = new Font(fontTypeface, Settings.Default.FontSubtitleSize, FontStyle.Italic);
        fontTitle = new Font(fontTypeface, Settings.Default.FontTitleSize, FontStyle.Bold);

        SizeF sizeTextAuthor = graphics.MeasureString(bookAuthor, fontAuthor);
        SizeF sizeTextDraft = graphics.MeasureString(bookDraftText, fontDraft);
        SizeF sizeTextSubtitle = graphics.MeasureString(bookSubtitle, fontSubtitle);
        SizeF sizeTextTitle = graphics.MeasureString(bookTitle, fontTitle);

        PointF pointTextTitle = new PointF(rectSafe.X + ((rectSafe.Width - sizeTextTitle.Width) / 2), rectSafe.Top + spacingTitle);
        PointF pointTextAuthor = new PointF(
            rectSafe.X + ((rectSafe.Width - sizeTextAuthor.Width) / 2),
            pointTextTitle.Y + spacingAuthor);
```

```csharp
            PointF pointTextSubtitle = new PointF(
                rectSafe.X + ((rectSafe.Width - sizeTextSubtitle.Width) / 2),
                pointTextAuthor.Y + spacingSubtitle);
            PointF pointTextDraft = new PointF(
                rectSafe.X + ((rectSafe.Width - sizeTextDraft.Width) / 2),
                pointTextSubtitle.Y + spacingDraft);

            // Draw the text on the Front Cover
            graphics.DrawStringEmbossed(bookTitle, fontTitle, Brushes.White, pointTextTitle, sizeTextTitle);
            graphics.DrawStringEmbossed(bookAuthor, fontAuthor, Brushes.White, pointTextAuthor, sizeTextAuthor);
            graphics.DrawStringEmbossed(bookSubtitle, fontSubtitle, Brushes.White, pointTextSubtitle, sizeTextSubtitle);
            if (Settings.Default.ShowDraft)
            {
                // Puts the draft text on the front cover
                graphics.DrawStringEmbossed(bookDraftText, fontDraft, Brushes.Black, pointTextDraft, sizeTextDraft);
            }
        }
        finally
        {
            fontTitle?.Dispose();
            fontAuthor?.Dispose();
            fontSubtitle?.Dispose();
            fontDraft?.Dispose();
        }
    }

    /// <summary>Adds a spine text.</summary>
    /// <param name="graphics">The graphics object to draw to.</param>
    /// <param name="dpi">The DPI of the cover.</param>
    /// <param name="rectSafe">The spine safe rectangle.</param>
    private static void AddSpineText(Graphics graphics, int dpi, RectangleF rectSafe)
    {
        Contract.Requires<ArgumentNullException>(graphics != null);

        Font fontTitleSpine = null;
        Font fontAuthorSpine = null;

        try
```

```
{
    string fontTypeface = Settings.Default.FontTypeface;
    string bookTitle = Settings.Default.BookTitle;
    string bookAuthor = Settings.Default.BookAuthor;
    float marginText = Settings.Default.MarginTextInches * dpi;

    fontTitleSpine = new Font(fontTypeface, Settings.Default.FontTitleSpineSize);
    fontAuthorSpine = new Font(fontTypeface, Settings.Default.FontAuthorSpineSize);

    SizeF sizeTextTitleSpine = graphics.MeasureString(bookTitle, fontTitleSpine);
    SizeF sizeTextAuthorSpine = graphics.MeasureString(bookAuthor, fontAuthorSpine);

    using (StringFormat stringFormat = new StringFormat(StringFormatFlags.DirectionVertical))
    {
        RectangleF rectTitleSpine = new RectangleF(
            rectSafe.X + ((rectSafe.Width - sizeTextTitleSpine.Height) / 2),
            rectSafe.Y + marginText,
            sizeTextTitleSpine.Height,
            sizeTextTitleSpine.Width);
        graphics.DrawStringEmbossed(bookTitle, fontTitleSpine, Brushes.White, rectTitleSpine, stringFormat);

        RectangleF rectAuthorSpine = new RectangleF(
            rectSafe.X + ((rectSafe.Width - sizeTextAuthorSpine.Height) / 2),
            rectSafe.Bottom - marginText - sizeTextAuthorSpine.Width,
            sizeTextAuthorSpine.Height,
            sizeTextAuthorSpine.Width);
        graphics.DrawStringEmbossed(bookAuthor, fontAuthorSpine, Brushes.White, rectAuthorSpine, stringFormat);
    }
}
finally
{
    fontTitleSpine?.Dispose();
    fontAuthorSpine?.Dispose();
}

/// <summary>Adds text and images to the background image.</summary>
/// <param name="graphics">The graphics object to draw to.</param>
```

```csharp
/// <param name="sizeCover">The cover size including bleed area.</param>
/// <param name="dpi">The DPI of the cover.</param>
/// <param name="sizeBookTrim">The book trim size.</param>
/// <param name="spineThickness">The spine thickness.</param>
/// <param name="sizeBleed">Size of the bleed area around the trim.</param>
private static void AddTextAndImages(
    Graphics graphics,
    Size sizeCover,
    int dpi,
    SizeF sizeBookTrim,
    float spineThickness,
    float sizeBleed)
{
    Contract.Requires<ArgumentNullException>(graphics != null);

    float marginSafe = Settings.Default.MarginSafeInches * dpi;
    float marginSafeSpine = Settings.Default.MarginSafeSpineInches * dpi;

    RectangleF rectTrim = new RectangleF(
        sizeBleed,
        sizeBleed,
        sizeCover.Width - (sizeBleed * 2),
        sizeCover.Height - (sizeBleed * 2));

    RectangleF rectSpine = new RectangleF(rectTrim.X + sizeBookTrim.Width, 0, spineThickness, sizeCover.Height);

    RectangleF rectSafeBack = new RectangleF(
        rectTrim.X + marginSafe,
        rectTrim.Y + marginSafe,
        sizeBookTrim.Width - (marginSafe * 2),
        sizeBookTrim.Height - (marginSafe * 2));

    RectangleF rectSafeSpine = new RectangleF(
        rectSpine.X + marginSafeSpine,
        rectTrim.X + marginSafeSpine,
        rectSpine.Width - (marginSafeSpine * 2),
        rectTrim.Height - (marginSafeSpine * 2));
```

```
RectangleF rectSafeFront = new RectangleF(
    rectSpine.Right + marginSafe,
    rectTrim.Y + marginSafe,
    sizeBookTrim.Width - (marginSafe * 2),
    sizeBookTrim.Height - (marginSafe * 2));

if (Settings.Default.ShowTrim)
{
    // Draw the trim rectangles
    using (Pen penGreen = new Pen(Color.Green, dpi / 150))
    {
        graphics.DrawRectangle(penGreen, rectTrim.X, rectTrim.Y, rectTrim.Width, rectTrim.Height);
        graphics.DrawRectangle(penGreen, rectSpine.X, rectSpine.Y, rectSpine.Width, rectSpine.Height);
    }
}

if (Settings.Default.ShowSafe)
{
    // Draw the safe area rectangles (areas where text cannot appear)
    using (Pen penBlue = new Pen(Color.Blue, dpi / 150))
    {
        graphics.DrawRectangle(penBlue, rectSafeBack.X, rectSafeBack.Y, rectSafeBack.Width, rectSafeBack.Height);
        graphics.DrawRectangle(penBlue, rectSafeSpine.X, rectSafeSpine.Y, rectSafeSpine.Width, rectSafeSpine.Height);
        graphics.DrawRectangle(penBlue, rectSafeFront.X, rectSafeFront.Y, rectSafeFront.Width, rectSafeFront.Height);
    }
}

Program.AddFrontCoverText(graphics, dpi, rectSafeFront);
Program.AddSpineText(graphics, dpi, rectSafeSpine);
Program.AddBackCoverText(graphics, dpi, rectSafeBack);

/// <summary>Creates a PDF of the cover from the bitmap using PDFSharp.</summary>
/// <param name="image">The image.</param>
/// <returns>The new space PDF.</returns>
private static string CreateSpacePdf(Image image)
{
    Contract.Requires<ArgumentNullException>(image != null);
```

```csharp
using (PdfDocument pdfDocument = new PdfDocument())
{
    Contract.Assume(pdfDocument.Info != null);
    pdfDocument.Info.Title = Settings.Default.BookTitle;
    pdfDocument.Info.Author = Settings.Default.BookAuthor;
    pdfDocument.Info.CreationDate = DateTime.Now;
    pdfDocument.Info.ModificationDate = DateTime.Now;
    pdfDocument.Info.Creator = AssemblyInfo.Attribute<AssemblyTitleAttribute>()?.Title;
    pdfDocument.Info.Subject = Settings.Default.BookSubtitle;

    // Create an empty page
    PdfPage pdfPage = pdfDocument.AddPage();
    Contract.Assume(pdfPage != null);
    pdfPage.Orientation = PdfSharp.PageOrientation.Landscape;
    pdfPage.Height = XUnit.FromInch(image.Height / image.VerticalResolution);
    pdfPage.Width = XUnit.FromInch(image.Width / image.HorizontalResolution);

    // Draw the bitmap on the page
    XGraphics xgraphics = XGraphics.FromPdfPage(pdfPage);
    XImage ximage = XImage.FromGdiPlusImage(image);
    xgraphics.DrawImage(ximage, 0, 0);

    // Save the document...
    string fileName = Path.Combine(Path.GetTempPath(), Settings.Default.CreateSpaceFileName);
    pdfDocument.Save(fileName);

    return fileName;
}

/// <summary>Gets an encoder for the particular ImageFormat.</summary>
/// <param name="imageFormat">Describes the image format to use.</param>
/// <returns>The encoder for the ImageFormat passed in.</returns>
private static ImageCodecInfo GetEncoder(ImageFormat imageFormat)
{
    Contract.Requires<ArgumentNullException>(imageFormat != null);
```

```csharp
            ImageCodecInfo result = null;

            ImageCodecInfo[] imageDecoders = ImageCodecInfo.GetImageDecoders();
            Contract.Assume(imageDecoders != null);
            foreach (ImageCodecInfo imageCodecInfo in imageDecoders)
            {
                Contract.Assume(imageCodecInfo != null);
                if (imageCodecInfo.FormatID == imageFormat.Guid)
                {
                    result = imageCodecInfo;
                    break;
                }
            }

            return result;
        }

        /// <summary>Makes create space cover.</summary>
        /// <param name="rhombusTiler">The rhombus tiler.</param>
        /// <param name="sizeBookTrimInches">The size book trim inches.</param>
        private static void MakeCreateSpaceCover(RhombusTiler rhombusTiler, SizeF sizeBookTrimInches)
        {
            Contract.Requires<ArgumentNullException>(rhombusTiler != null);

            int dpi = Settings.Default.CreateSpaceDpi;
            float marginBleed = Settings.Default.MarginBleedInches * dpi;
            SizeF sizeBookTrim = new SizeF(sizeBookTrimInches.Width * dpi, sizeBookTrimInches.Height * dpi);
            float spineThickness = Program.PageThicknessInches * Settings.Default.BookPageCount * dpi;

            Size sizeCover = new Size(
                (int)(((sizeBookTrim.Width + marginBleed) * 2) + spineThickness),
                (int)(sizeBookTrim.Height + (marginBleed * 2)));

            // Get the background image
            using (Bitmap bitmap = rhombusTiler.GetBitmap(sizeCover, dpi))
            {
                using (Graphics graphics = Graphics.FromImage(bitmap))
                {
```

```
            // Add the elements to the image
            Program.AddTextAndImages(
                graphics,
                bitmap.Size,
                dpi,
                sizeBookTrim,
                spineThickness,
                marginBleed);
        }

        // Create the pdf
        string fileName = Program.CreateSpacePdf(bitmap);

        // View the pdf
        Process.Start(fileName);
    }

    /// <summary>Makes kindle cover.</summary>
    /// <param name="rhombusTiler">The rhombus tiler.</param>
    /// <param name="sizeBookTrimInches">The size book trim inches.</param>
    private static void MakeKindleCover(RhombusTiler rhombusTiler, SizeF sizeBookTrimInches)
    {
        Contract.Requires<ArgumentNullException>(rhombusTiler != null);

        int kindleHeight = Settings.Default.KindleHeight;
        float kindleAspectRatio = Settings.Default.KindleAspectRatio;
        Size sizeCoverKindle = new Size((int)Math.Ceiling(kindleHeight / kindleAspectRatio), kindleHeight);
        int dpiKindle = (int)(kindleHeight / sizeBookTrimInches.Height);

        // Get the background image
        using (Bitmap bitmap = rhombusTiler.GetBitmap(sizeCoverKindle, dpiKindle))
        {
            using (Graphics graphics = Graphics.FromImage(bitmap))
            {
                float marginSafe = Settings.Default.MarginSafeInches * dpiKindle;
                RectangleF rectSafeFront = new RectangleF(
                    marginSafe,
```

```csharp
                marginSafe,
                bitmap.Width - (marginSafe * 2),
                bitmap.Height - (marginSafe * 2));

            Program.AddFrontCoverText(graphics, dpiKindle, rectSafeFront);
        }

        dpiKindle = Settings.Default.KindleDpi;
        bitmap.SetResolution(dpiKindle, dpiKindle);

        // Save the file with no compression, a Kindle requirement
        Contract.Assume(Settings.Default.KindleFileName != null);
        Contract.Assume(Settings.Default.KindleImageFormat != null);
        string fileNameKindle = Path.Combine(Path.GetTempPath(), Settings.Default.KindleFileName);
        ImageCodecInfo imageCodecInfo = GetEncoder(Settings.Default.KindleImageFormat);
        using (EncoderParameters encoderParameters = new EncoderParameters(1))
        {
            Contract.Assume(encoderParameters.Param != null);
            Contract.Assume(encoderParameters.Param.Length == 1);
            encoderParameters.Param[0] = new EncoderParameter(Encoder.Quality, 100L);
            bitmap.Save(fileNameKindle, imageCodecInfo, encoderParameters);
        }

        // View the file
        Process.Start(fileNameKindle);
        }
    }
}
```

Xoc.Penrose\Properties\AssemblyInfo.cs

```csharp
//-------------------------------------------------------------------------
// <copyright file="AssemblyInfo.cs" company="Xoc Software">
// Copyright © 2015 Xoc Software
// </copyright>
// <summary>Implements the assembly information class</summary>
//-------------------------------------------------------------------------
using System;
```

```
using System.Diagnostics.Contracts;
using System.Reflection;
using System.Resources;
using System.Runtime.InteropServices;

[assembly: AssemblyCompany("Xoc Software")]
#if DEBUG
[assembly: AssemblyConfiguration("Debug")]
#else
[assembly: AssemblyConfiguration("Release")]
#endif
[assembly: AssemblyCopyright("Copyright © 2015 Xoc Software")]
[assembly: AssemblyDelaySign(false)]
[assembly: AssemblyDescription("Creates a Penrose Tiling Bitmap.")]
[assembly: AssemblyInformationalVersion("1.0")]
[assembly: AssemblyProduct("Xoc.Penrose")]
[assembly: AssemblyTitle("Xoc Penrose Tiler")]
[assembly: AssemblyTrademark("Xoc is a trademark of Xoc Software")]
[assembly: AssemblyVersion("1.0.*")]
[assembly: CLSCompliant(true)]
[assembly: ComVisible(false)]
[assembly: ContractVerification(true)]
[assembly: Guid("22909ce5-e3e1-441e-ac8e-be93e8af89b6")]
[assembly: NeutralResourcesLanguage("en-US")]
```

Xoc.Penrose\RhombusTiler.cs

```
// <copyright file="RhombusTiler.cs" company="Xoc Software" >
// Copyright © 2015 Xoc Software
// </copyright>
// <summary>Implements the rhombus tiler class</summary>
//
namespace Xoc.Penrose
{
    using System;
    using System.Collections.ObjectModel;
    using System.Diagnostics;
    using System.Diagnostics.CodeAnalysis;
```

```csharp
using System.Diagnostics.Contracts;
using System.Drawing;
using System.Drawing.Drawing2D;
using System.Drawing.Imaging;

/// <summary>A rhombus tiler.</summary>
public class RhombusTiler
{
    /// <summary>Establish the number of initial spokes to the wheel.</summary>
    private const int Spokes = 10;

    /// <summary>Initializes a new instance of the <see cref="RhombusTiler"/> class..</summary>
    /// <param name="iterations">The iterations.</param>
    public RhombusTiler(int iterations)
    {
        // Initialize wheel
        PointF a = new PointF(0, 0);
        for (int i = 0; i < Spokes; i++)
        {
            int reverse = i % 2 == 0 ? 1 : -1;
            PointF b = RhombusTiler.PolarToCartesian(1, (float)(((2 * i) - reverse) * Math.PI / Spokes));
            PointF c = RhombusTiler.PolarToCartesian(1, (float)(((2 * i) + reverse) * Math.PI / Spokes));
            Triangle triangle = new Triangle(RhombusType.Fat, a, b, c);
            this.Triangles.Add(triangle);
        }

        for (int i = 0; i < iterations; i++)
        {
            Collection<Triangle> newSet = new Collection<Triangle>();
            foreach (Triangle triangle in this.Triangles)
            {
                Collection<Triangle> subdivided = triangle.Subdivide();
                foreach (Triangle newTriangle in subdivided)
                {
                    newSet.Add(newTriangle);
                }
            }
```

```csharp
        this.Triangles = newSet;
    }
}

/// <summary>Gets the triangles.</summary>
/// <value>The triangles.</value>
private Collection<Triangle> Triangles
{
    get;
} = new Collection<Triangle>();

/// <summary>Gets a bitmap with the Penrose tiling in it.</summary>
/// <param name="size">The size.</param>
/// <param name="dpi">The DPI.</param>
/// <returns>The bitmap. The caller must dispose the bitmap.</returns>
[SuppressMessage("Microsoft.Reliability", "CA2000:Dispose objects before losing scope", Justification = "Returns bitmap")]
public Bitmap GetBitmap(Size size, int dpi)
{
    Contract.Ensures(Contract.Result<Bitmap>() != null);
    Contract.Ensures((Contract.Result<Bitmap>().PixelFormat & PixelFormat.Indexed) == 0);

    Bitmap bitmap = new Bitmap(size.Width, size.Height, PixelFormat.Format32bppRgb);
    bitmap.SetResolution(dpi, dpi);
    Contract.Assume((bitmap.PixelFormat & PixelFormat.Indexed) == 0);
    using (Graphics graphics = Graphics.FromImage(bitmap))
    {
        using (Pen pen = new Pen(Brushes.Black, (float)Math.Ceiling(dpi / 150d)))
        {
            foreach (Triangle triangle in this.Triangles)
            {
                triangle.DrawTriangle(graphics, size, 10000f * (float)Math.Ceiling(dpi / 300d), pen);
            }
        }

        Rectangle rect = new Rectangle(0, 0, size.Width, size.Height);
        LinearGradientBrush linearGradientBrush = new LinearGradientBrush(
            rect,
            Color.FromArgb(64, Color.Black),
```

```
                Color.FromArgb(0, Color.Black),
                LinearGradientMode.Vertical);

            graphics.FillRectangle(linearGradientBrush, rect);
        }

        Contract.Assume((bitmap.PixelFormat & PixelFormat.Indexed) == 0);
        return bitmap;
    }

    /// <summary>Polar to cartesian coordinate changer.</summary>
    /// <param name="radius">The polar radius.</param>
    /// <param name="angle">The polar angle in radians.</param>
    /// <returns>A PointF.</returns>
    private static PointF PolarToCartesian(float radius, float angle)
    {
        return new PointF((float)(radius * Math.Cos(angle)), (float)(radius * Math.Sin(angle)));
    }

    /// <summary>Object invariant.</summary>
    [Conditional("CONTRACTS_FULL")]
    [ContractInvariantMethod]
    [SuppressMessage("Microsoft.Performance", "CA1822:MarkMembersAsStatic", Justification = "Invariant can't be static.")]
    private void ZzObjectInvariant()
    {
        Contract.Invariant(this.Triangles != null);
    }
    }
}
```

Xoc.Penrose\RhombusType.cs

```
//-------------------------------------
// <copyright file="RhombusType.cs" company="Xoc Software">
// Copyright © 2015 Xoc Software
// </copyright>
// <summary>Implements the rhombus type class</summary>
//-------------------------------------
namespace Xoc.Penrose
```

```
        /// <summary>Values that represent Penrose rhombuses.</summary>
        internal enum RhombusType
        {
            /// <summary>The "fat" rhombus.</summary>
            Fat,

            /// <summary>The "thin" rhombus.</summary>
            Thin
        }
    }
```

Xoc.Penrose\Triangle.cs

```
//--------------------------------------------------------------
// <copyright file="Triangle.cs" company="Xoc Software">
// Copyright © 2015 Xoc Software
// </copyright>
// <summary>Implements the triangle class</summary>
//--------------------------------------------------------------
namespace Xoc.Penrose
{
    using System;
    using System.Collections.ObjectModel;
    using System.Diagnostics.Contracts;
    using System.Drawing;

    /// <summary>A triangle.</summary>
    internal class Triangle
    {
        /// <summary>The fat rhombus brush.</summary>
        private static readonly Brush BrushFatRhombus = new SolidBrush(Color.FromArgb(0x83, 0x15, 0x18));

        /// <summary>The thin rhombus brush.</summary>
        private static readonly Brush BrushThinRhombus = new SolidBrush(Color.FromArgb(0xb3, 0x1c, 0x1f));

        /// <summary>The Golden ratio.</summary>
        private static readonly float Phi = (float)((1 + Math.Sqrt(5)) / 2);
```

```csharp
        /// <summary>The offset.</summary>
        private PointF offset;

        /// <summary>The scale.</summary>
        private float scale;

        /// <summary>
        /// Initializes a new instance of the
        /// <see cref="Triangle"/> class.
        /// </summary>
        /// <param name="penroseRhombus">The type of the rhombus (fat or thin).</param>
        /// <param name="a">The A corner of the triangle.</param>
        /// <param name="b">The B corner of the triangle.</param>
        /// <param name="c">The C corner of the triangle.</param>
        internal Triangle(RhombusType penroseRhombus, PointF a, PointF b, PointF c)
        {
            this.RhombusType = penroseRhombus;
            this.A = a;
            this.B = b;
            this.C = c;
        }

        /// <summary>Gets or sets the A corner of the triangle.</summary>
        /// <value>The A corner of the triangle.</value>
        internal PointF A
        {
            get;
            set;
        } = new PointF(0, 0);

        /// <summary>Gets or sets the B corner of the triangle.</summary>
        /// <value>The B corner of the triangle.</value>
        internal PointF B
        {
            get;
            set;
        } = new PointF(0, 0);
```

239

```
/// <summary>Gets or sets the C corner of the triangle.</summary>
/// <value>The C corner of the triangle.</value>
internal PointF C
{
    get;
    set;
} = new PointF(0, 0);

/// <summary>Gets or sets the type of rhombus, fat or thin.</summary>
/// <value>The type of the rhombus.</value>
internal RhombusType RhombusType
{
    get;
    set;
} = RhombusType.Fat;

/// <summary>Gets the scaled value of the A corner of the rectangle.</summary>
/// <value>The A corner scaled.</value>
private PointF AScale
{
    get
    {
        return new PointF((this.A.X * this.scale) + this.offset.X, (this.A.Y * this.scale) + this.offset.Y);
    }
}

/// <summary>Gets the scaled value of the B corner of the rectangle.</summary>
/// <value>The B corner scaled.</value>
private PointF BScale
{
    get
    {
        return new PointF((this.B.X * this.scale) + this.offset.X, (this.B.Y * this.scale) + this.offset.Y);
    }
}

/// <summary>Gets the scaled value of the C corner of the rectangle.</summary>
/// <value>The C corner scaled.</value>
```

```csharp
private PointF CScale
{
    get
    {
        return new PointF((this.C.X * this.scale) + this.offset.X, (this.C.Y * this.scale) + this.offset.Y);
    }
}

/// <summary>Draw the triangle.</summary>
/// <param name="graphics">The graphics object to draw on.</param>
/// <param name="bitmapSize">Size of the bitmap.</param>
/// <param name="scaleImage">The scale of the image.</param>
/// <param name="pen">The pen.</param>
internal void DrawTriangle(Graphics graphics, Size bitmapSize, float scaleImage, Pen pen)
{
    Contract.Requires<ArgumentNullException>(graphics != null);

    this.scale = scaleImage;
    this.offset = new PointF(bitmapSize.Width / 2, bitmapSize.Height / 2);

    Brush brush;

    switch (this.RhombusType)
    {
        default:
        case RhombusType.Fat:
            brush = Triangle.BrushFatRhombus;
            break;
        case RhombusType.Thin:
            brush = Triangle.BrushThinRhombus;
            break;
    }

    PointF[] points = new PointF[] { this.AScale, this.BScale, this.CScale };

    graphics.DrawPolygon(pen, points);
    graphics.FillPolygon(brush, points);
}
```

```csharp
/// <summary>Gets the triangle subdivided into two or three smaller triangles.</summary>
/// <returns>A Collection of Triangles.</returns>
internal Collection<Triangle> Subdivide()
{
    Collection<Triangle> result = new Collection<Triangle>();

    switch (this.RhombusType)
    {
        default:
        case RhombusType.Fat:
            PointF p = new PointF(this.A.X + ((this.B.X - this.A.X) / Phi), this.A.Y + ((this.B.Y - this.A.Y) / Phi));
            result.Add(new Triangle(RhombusType.Fat, this.C, p, this.B));
            result.Add(new Triangle(RhombusType.Thin, p, this.C, this.A));
            break;
        case RhombusType.Thin:
            PointF q = new PointF(this.B.X + ((this.A.X - this.B.X) / Phi), this.B.Y + ((this.A.Y - this.B.Y) / Phi));
            PointF r = new PointF(this.B.X + ((this.C.X - this.B.X) / Phi), this.B.Y + ((this.C.Y - this.B.Y) / Phi));
            result.Add(new Triangle(RhombusType.Thin, r, this.C, this.B));
            result.Add(new Triangle(RhombusType.Thin, q, r, this.B));
            result.Add(new Triangle(RhombusType.Fat, r, q, this.A));
            break;
    }

    return result;
}
```

REFERENCES AND RESOURCES

The URLs are current as of the time of publication.

Abrams, Brad. "Internal Coding Guidelines," http://blogs.msdn.com/b/brada/archive/2005/01/26/361363.aspx.

Alvestrand, H. "RFC 1766:Tags for the Identification of Languages," https://tools.ietf.org/html/rfc1766.

Bradner, Scott. "RFC 2119: Key Words for Use in RFCs to Indicate Requirement Levels," https://tools.ietf.org/html/rfc2119.

"Circular 3, Copyright Notice," http://www.copyright.gov/circs/circ03.pdf.

"C# Language Specification 5.0." *Microsoft Download Center*, https://www.microsoft.com/en-us/download/details.aspx?id=7029.

"C# Language Specification for Asynchronous Functions." *Microsoft Download Center*, https://www.microsoft.com/en-us/download/details.aspx?id=23753.

"Code Contracts - Microsoft Research," http://research.microsoft.com/en-us/projects/contracts.

"Code Contracts User Manual." Microsoft Corporation, https://research.microsoft.com/en-us/projects/contracts/userdoc.pdf.

"Code Conventions for the Java™ Programming Language." Oracle Corporation, http://www.oracle.com/technetwork/java/javase/documentation/codeconvtoc-136057.html.

"Code Signing Best Practices." Microsoft Corporation, http://www.microsoft.com/whdc/winlogo/drvsign/best_practices.mspx.

"Coding Guidelines for C# 3.0, C# 4.0 and C# 5.0," https://csharpguidelines.codeplex.com/releases/view/46280.

Cwalina, Krzysztof, and Brad Abrams. *Framework Design Guidelines: Conventions, Idioms, and Patterns for Reusable .NET Libraries. 2nd Edition.* Upper Saddle River, NJ: Addison-Wesley, 2008.

"Design Guidelines for Developing Class Libraries," https://msdn.microsoft.com/library/ms229042(v=vs.100).aspx.

"Extensible Markup Language (XML) 1.1 (Second Edition)," http://www.w3.org/TR/2006/REC-xml11-20060816.

"FxCop 10.0." *Microsoft Download Center*, https://www.microsoft.com/en-us/download/details.aspx?id=6544.

"FxCop Design Warnings," https://msdn.microsoft.com/en-us/library/ms182125(v=vs.100).aspx.

"Google Java Style." Google, https://google.github.io/styleguide/javaguide.html.

"IDesign Coding Standards," http://www.idesign.net/Downloads/GetDownload/1985.

"Indent Style." *Wikipedia, the Free Encyclopedia*, https://en.wikipedia.org/wiki/Indent_style.

Krüger, Mike. "C# Coding Style Guide." ic#code, http://www.icsharpcode.net/TechNotes/SharpDevelopCodingStyle03.pdf.

"Microsoft All-In-One Code Framework," https://1code.codeplex.com/wikipage?title=All-In-One%20Code%20Framework%20Coding%20Standards.

Reddick, Greg. "Greg Reddick's Blog," http://blog.xoc.net.

"RFC 3305:URIs, URLs, and URNs: Clarifications and Recommendations Report from the Joint W3C/IETF URI Planning Interest Group," https://tools.ietf.org/html/rfc3305.

"Standard ECMA-334 C# Language Specification 4th Edition," http://www.ecma-international.org/publications/standards/Ecma-334.htm.

"StyleCop." *CodePlex*, https://stylecop.codeplex.com/Wikipage?ProjectName=stylecop.

"StyleCop+." *CodePlex*, https://stylecopplus.codeplex.com/Wikipage?ProjectName=stylecopplus.

"StyleCop Rules," http://www.stylecop.com/docs/StyleCop Rules.html.

von Ballmoos, Marco, Remo von Ballmoos, and Marc Dürst. "Encodo C# Handbook." Encodo Systems AG., http://encodo.com/assets/pdfs/Encodo-CSharp-Handbook.pdf.

INDEX

COLOPHON

About the Author

Greg Reddick has been a software engineer for more than 35 years. He is the owner of Xoc Software, a software development and training company. He has a B.S. in Computer Information Systems. As a Software Design Engineer at Microsoft, he wrote part of Microsoft Access 1.0. Greg has co-authored a number of books and videos on Microsoft .NET and Microsoft Access.

Since 1994, Greg has provided training on various aspects of programming and web development.

When not programming, Greg studies the ancient Maya culture (see https://mayacalendar.xoc.net), dances Argentine tango, folds proteins on Foldit, and sails on Lake Washington (see http://www.yachtslog.com).

He maintains his blog at http://blog.xoc.net.

Colophon

This book was written in Microsoft Word. In the print version of the book, the main text is in the Cambria typeface. The code examples are in the Consolas. References to code in the text are in Gill Sans MT. Special characters in the text, such as ✓, are in Arial Unicode MS. In electronic editions of the book, the typefaces may vary.

The pattern on the cover is a Penrose Tiling, a kind of non-periodic tiling. (https://en.wikipedia.org/wiki/Penrose_tiling)

Geralyne Rudolph designed the Xoc Software logo and the graphic layout for this book.

Made in the USA
Coppell, TX
13 May 2024

32371753R00144